The Jill Tars

The Jill Tars

Seven Remarkable Accounts of Female Sailors
Who Served and Fought Disguised as Men

Rachel Beatty

LEONAUR

The Jill Tars
Seven Remarkable Accounts of Female Sailors Who Served and Fought Disguised as Men
By Rachel Beatty

FIRST EDITION

Leonaur is an imprint of Oakpast Ltd

Copyright in this form © 2015 Oakpast Ltd

ISBN: 978-1-78282-465-7 (hardcover)
ISBN: 978-1-78282-466-4 (softcover)

http://www.leonaur.com

Contents

The Intrepid Female: or, Surprising Life and Adventures of Mary Ann Talbot, Otherwise John Taylor

Related by Herself

I was born to experience a large portion of the disagreeable circumstances incident to human nature; and if the reader of the following pages should judge harshly the inducements that precipitated me into the early part of the misfortunes which have attended each succeeding year of my life, I have only to supplicate commiseration towards a being bred in a country village, and from thence sent to a boarding-school 180 miles from the metropolis, on leaving which, after nine years careful attention to my education and morals, I have to date the commencement of my future troubles.

I am the youngest of sixteen natural children, which my mother had by Lord William Talbot, Baron of Hensol, steward of His Majesty's household, and colonel of the Glamorganshire militia, with whom she kept a secret correspondence for several years. I never could trace any particular event taking place at my birth, which might serve as a presage of the singular adventures which I have since met with; unless it was the circumstance of my being a surviving twin, nor do I know anything relative to the juvenile part of my life, but from the information of an only sister considerably elder than myself, and whom indeed I had taken to be my mother.

From her I learnt I was born in London, in the parish of St. Giles, on the 2nd day of Feb. 1778, in the house now in part occupied by Mr. Gosling, the banker, in Lincoln's Inn Fields. The hour which brought me into the world deprived me of the fostering care of a mother, whose loss I can never sufficiently regret, and in a short time I was sent to nurse at a small village called Worthin, about twelve miles from Shrewsbury, where I remained until I had attained my fifth year, under the fostering care of an excellent woman, without feeling the irreparable loss I had sustained in the death of the only parent who might have been my protector and guide through life.

At the expiration of my fifth year I was removed, (I know not by whose orders, but rather imagine by some friend of Earl Talbot's, who died before I left my nurse) to Mrs. Tapperly's boarding-school, Foregate-street, Chester, in order to receive a liberal education. Here I remained nine years, unacquainted with the vices of the world, and knew no misery but seeing children more fortunate than myself, receiving the embraces of their parents and friends. During my residence at Mrs. Tapperly's, I found a kind protector in my only surviving sister, who was married to a Mr. Wilson of Trevalyn, in the county of Denbigh, North-Wales.

In this relative I found every attention and care expected from a parent, and whom, indeed, as I have before stated, I took to be such. In her society I enjoyed the only gleam of happiness I was doomed to experience, from the instant of my coming into the world to the present instant; and even this was but of short duration; for alas, in the bloom of her youth, and the flower of her age, she unfortunately fall a victim to childbirth, leaving me to regret, by the same visitation of Providence, a second parent, in the loss of a sister and friend united, and whom I tenderly loved; and as such, have never ceased to lament. She told me the name she was known by before her marriage, was the Hon. Miss Dyer, being the name of the family she was brought up in; and that she possessed a fortune of 30,000l. besides an income of fifteen hundred pounds *per annum*.

Deprived thus of the only relation and friend whom I knew in the world; and at an age too when I stood most in need of her advice and assistance, I felt a vacuity in my heart, which rendered existence irksome. The care of me now devolved solely on a gentleman of the name of Sucker, who resided at Newport in the county of Salop, who within three months after the decease of my sister, taking on himself the authority of a guardian, removed me from the school at Chester, and placed me in his own family, where I soon became sensible of the loss I had sustained in the death of my dear sister, in a more eminent degree than ever; as the severity of Mr. Sucker seldom permitted me to quit the room assigned me but at meal-times; and seemed by the general conduct of his manners, to inspire me with a dread of his person, and consequently to avoid as much as possible any conversation on my circumstances, or that of my deceased sister. I must confess I was at a loss during the period I resided with him, to assign any reason for his conduct towards me; but have since been so perfectly satisfied as to its being a premeditated plan of his, to throw me in the way of any person whatever, who would remove from his care a charge, that, for reasons only known to himself, was intolerable.

I had not long been under the roof of this inhospitable man, before he introduced me to Captain Essex Bowen of the 82nd Regiment of Foot, whom I had once before seen at Chester, in company with Mr. Sucker; and understood from him, was then on the recruiting service. This was about a week previous to my quitting Mrs. Tapperly's, and who now appeared to be well acquainted with the particulars of my birth and family.

From the moment of his introduction to me at Mr. Sucker's, he paid me particular attention, which I accounted for in consequence of Mr. Sucker's observing—I was to consider him as my future guardian, he being appointed to superintend my education abroad; and requested me to pay him every possible regard, as the person to whose care I was entrusted.

In a few days I quitted Mr. Sucker's in company with Captain Bowen, who, on our departure, pretended to my late guardian, the most inviolable attachment to my family; and assured him in my hearing, that he would on his arrival in town, place me under the care of a female friend, in order to complete my education, and knowledge of the world; without which, he declared I should be considered as an alien by my own family.

Unexperienced in the ways of a deceitful world, my youthful mind was elated at the thoughts of visiting London, a place which I had heard so much talk of, and was highly delighted with the varying scenes which alternately presented themselves to my view on the road, though the season of the year was rather inauspicious to beautiful prospects, being in January, 1792. On our arrival in the capital, which we reached without any remarkable circumstance, I was conveyed by Captain Bowen to the Salopian coffee-house, Charing-Cross, kept at that time by a Mrs. Wright, to whom I was introduced as his charge; and where I soon after experienced a visible change in the manners of my pretended protector; who in a very short period put in practice the villainous scheme which he had, no doubt, before our arrival in town, premeditatedly resolved on.

Instead of exhibiting the least remorse, or endeavouring to soothe a mind, agitated by his proceedings, he threw off the mask which had hitherto concealed the villain, and placed in my view the determined ruffian. Intimidated by his manners, and in the knowledge of no friend near me, I became everything he could desire; and so far aided his purposes as to become a willing instrument to my future misfortunes.

I did not remain long before I was to become the object of more degradation; as in consequence of an order from the regiment Captain Bowen belonged to, he was ordered to embark for St. Domingo, and projecting farther plans on my happiness, for, conceiving me properly subjugated to his purpose, and remarking that my figure was extremely well calculated for the situation he had assigned me, he produced a complete suit of male attire; and for the first time made me acquainted with the unmanly design he had formed, of taking me with him to the West-Indies, in the menial capacity of his foot-boy.

I had not much time to deliberate how to act; and by this time knowing his peremptory disposition, in a fit of frenzy and despair, I yielded to the base proposal, and assumed the character he had thought fit to assign me, together with the name of John Taylor, which I ever after retained.

Thus equipped, I travelled with him to Falmouth, where soon after our arrival, we embarked on board the Crown transport, *Captain Bishop*, and set sail for the West Indies on the 20th day of March, 1792. We had not been long on our voyage before I began to experience the hardships of my situation: shipboard even to the most robust and daring of the male sex, is at first a very unpleasant dwelling; and it must naturally be supposed, was to one like myself particularly disagreeable; and the novelty of my new attire did not exempt me from being compelled to live and mess with the most menial of the ship's company, as Captain Bowen never suffered me once after I was on board to eat with him, but forced me to put up with what he left at meal times.

Fearful of incurring the raillery which detection would have occasioned, I resolved to endure the hardships I suffered with patience, rather than discover my sex.

During our voyage we encountered a most tremendous gale, which continued several days with such fury, that we were obliged to throw our guns overboard, in order to lighten the ship, and were reduced to such distress, as to render it necessary for the pumps to be kept at work continually; in consequence of which every person without distinction, (officers excepted) was obliged to assist in the laborious office. It was in this extremity I first learnt the duty of a sailor; being obliged on some necessary occasion, first to go aloft, which frequent use rendered at last familiar, and by no means irksome.

In addition to our affliction, the storm having driven us several leagues out of our latitude, we were compelled to put ourselves on half allowance; having, in our eagerness to lighten the ship, thrown overboard, besides the guns, casks of water, bags of biscuits, and many articles of indispensible necessity to our future comfort, which we after severely missed; in consequence of which, we were compelled to put ourselves on the short allowance of a biscuit per day; and for water we were so much distressed as to be wholly without it for the space of eight days, during which period we were happy in consequence of some favourable showers, to wring the rainwater from our watch coats, which, on such occasions, we never failed to hand out, to retain as much as possible the providential succour received. Nay, to such extremity were we reduced for want of this necessary article of life, that I have gladly flown to any little settlement of water on the deck, eagerly to apply my lips to the boards to allay the parching thirst I experienced.

As if the measure of our troubles were not accomplished, our main-top-gallant mast was rent asunder, and swept four men busily engaged at the windlass for our mutual preservation, into the sea, whom we never saw more.

Whether in consequence of the agitation I underwent, in the exertion of what I conceived now my duty, or the want of necessary provision, I know not; but the sudden loss of appetite I experienced, threatened to bring on me a fit of illness. After the storm was abated, a strong gale sprung up, and being in favour of our course we proceeded at the rate of thirteen and fourteen knots an hour.

We arrived at Port-au-Prince in the island of St. Domingo, early in the month of June; where, after the fatigue and distress I suffered on the voyage, by fortunate opportunities of taking moderate rest, my health and spirits were quickly restored, except a little weakness and debility brought afterwards on by the heat of the climate, and occasional melancholy reflections on my own unfortunate situation; as during my continuance on this island I avoided as much as possible, the sight and company of my destructive and abandoned betrayer.

Our stay at St. Domingo was but of short duration, owing to the arrival of a packet from England, which missed overtaking us, with orders to countermand our destination, and to join the troops on the Continent, under the command of His Royal Highness the Duke of York, by the gale before described. Here it was I was doomed to undergo another change of character; for Captain Bowen, judging it not convenient to continue me in the situation of his foot-boy, proposed my being enrolled in the regiment as a drummer which, on my objecting to, he threatened to have me conveyed up the country, and sold as a slave. From the dread of his really putting his threat into execution, I reluctantly acquiesced in his desire, and was immediately equipped in the dress of a drummer, and learnt the art of beating the drum from the instructions of drum-major Rickardson.

In pursuance of the orders brought by the packet, we immediately embarked on board some transports appointed for that service; and, being favoured with a brisk gale during the best part of our voyage, we arrived in safety at the place of our destination, a port on the coast of Flanders, the name of which I cannot well remember; as immediately after our debarkation, we were marched off to join the main army at headquarters; previous to reaching which, I found I was to answer the purpose of Captain Bowen, as before, in the capacity of his drudge and foot-boy, whenever opportunity would allow the attendance from my duty as drummer. This mode of life was by no means congenial to my feelings; and, indeed, was in my eyes worse than the situation which I was in while foot-boy only, although I was more immediately compelled to endure the sight of a man, now rendered to me detestable.

I perfectly remember one, among a multitude of harassing excursions, which had nearly proved fatal to His Royal Highness the Duke of York, a part of his army, as well as to myself. After a long and heavy march of thirty miles in one day, without halting more than once for refreshment, while pitching our tents and making entrenchments, a part of our troops, for a time taking rest, were surprised and surrounded by the enemy, excepting a small space which led to an adjacent wood, and furnished a means of retreat to a part of the army, among which I was one, though without other apparel than my small clothes.

The enemy observing our camp at rest, made the attempt in the middle of the night, owing to which circumstances many others, as well as myself, were equally unprepared in point of accoutrements, though the most we suffered on this occasion was the alarm, as a large party of Austrians, who had doubtless watched the motions of our adversaries, came timely to our assistance, and compelled the unwelcome intruders to make a precipitate retreat, by which we regained our former station.

We continued to have frequent skirmishes with the enemy previous to the grand object of our royal commander, namely, the celebrated siege of Valenciennes, at which place I became subject to greater hardships than any that I had hitherto experienced. Compelled to remain among my comrades wherever duty called, in the various struggles which preceded the surrender of the place, an eyewitness to hundreds of friends and foes indiscriminately falling around me; where the 11th Dragoons, conspicuous above the rest, fought with their broadswords hand to hand, over heaps of dead and dying soldiers, I was shocked to see many a brave fellow at first but slightly wounded, meet his death by the trampling of horses, spurred on by the contending antagonists, during these conflicts, obliged to keep a continual roll to drown the cries and confusion on the various scenes of action. The infantry equally distinguished themselves; as, wherever the enemy, however superior in numbers, opposed their progress, they never failed to meet their fate on the point of the British bayonet.

Towards the end of this memorable siege, I received two wounds, though fortunately neither deep nor dangerous: the first from a musquet ball, which glancing between my breast and collar bone, struck my rib; and the other on the small of my back, from the broadsword of an Austrian trooper, which, I imagine, rather proceeded from accident than design, the marks of which two wounds I still bear. I carefully concealed them, from the dread of their discovering my sex, and effected a perfect cure, by the assistance of a little basilican, lint, and a few Dutch drops. These accidents happened on the same day the Hon. Mr. Tolemache was killed by a musquet ball.

Soon afterwards Valenciennes surrendered, and we in consequence marched in and took possession of the town, and found most of the women and children had taken refuge in cellars and places underground. I need scarcely notice, every possible protection was afforded to these unfortunate sufferers. On our arrival in the town I learnt that my persecutor, Captain Bowen, was no more, having fallen in the attack; this I was informed of by one of my comrades: and though I had every reason rather to rejoice at such an event than grieve, yet it was with the greatest difficulty I could smother the sudden emotion I experienced on the intelligence, or conceal the hidden character of a woman, in shedding a tear on his fate, however unworthy. I had no great difficulty in finding his body; nor was it thought strange I should endeavour to seek him out, being always in the habit of attending on him at his tent, when I was off duty.

I took from his pocket the key of his desk, out of which I took some letters, which on perusing in private, I found chiefly relating to myself; being the correspondence of my former guardian, Mr. Sucker: these I carefully preserved, and sewed up under the shoulder straps of my shirt.

I now felt my situation truly distressing; left in a strange country without a friend to consult, or a place where I could find an asylum, I suffered under the most poignant grief, at the same time labouring under excruciating pain, and my wounds so situated, that I durst not reveal them without a discovery of my sex, which I ever carefully avoided. I hazarded everything to keep inviolable my own secret, and committed the care of my wounds to my own single endeavour and the hand of time. Thus situated, I formed a resolution to desert from a duty at best imposed on me, and endeavour to return to England. This step I might not have thought on, had I not discovered by Mr. Sucker's letters that I had been grossly imposed on, as money had been remitted to Captain Bowen, and my name was mentioned in a way which gave rise to suspicions I had hitherto been a stranger to, and to explain how he had notwithstanding, treated me, was now my purpose to reveal

Having formed my plan, little time was necessary to put it in execution. I set out on foot that morning for the first place Providence might point out, as my deliverance from an enemy's country; however inexperienced I might be in some respects, I had the precaution to change my drummer's dress for one which I had been accustomed to wear when on board, and during a long part of my journey I carefully avoided any town, or place of considerable appearance; always on such occasions taking a circuitous route, frequently sleeping in a tree, under a haystack, and sometimes in places much less convenient.

The diminutive and insignificant figure which I made in my sailor's attire, served me, among the peasantry of the country villages I was under the necessity of passing to obtain refreshment from any straggling boy I could meet with on the skirts of the place, as a passport; for no one thought it worth their while to question a person of my mean appearance.

In this manner I arrived at Luxemburg in September, without experiencing the least molestation; here I soon found my ignorance in

14

political matters had led me into an error of a very awkward nature; and that being a town in possession of the French, they would not suffer me to proceed farther on my journey. Had I fortunately taken the contrary route, I should most probably have reached Dunkirk or Calais in one third of the time it occupied me, in traversing that part of the country; as I have learnt from persons conversant with the maps of the Continent, the distance from Valenciennes to either of the last mentioned parts, is small in comparison to that I had inadvertently taken to Luxemburg. Finding myself thus situated, destitute of every necessary of life, and in the midst of a country where no one paid me the smallest regard, I was constrained through mere necessity, though sorely against my wish, to engage with a Captain Le Sage, commander of a French lugger, on board which I embarked on the 17th of September, 1793.

Soon afterwards we dropped down the Rhine, and sailed on a cruise, when I was put to the most common drudgery of the vessel; but even this I could have borne with patience, had not the painful idea occurred to my mind, that in this new situation, I should be doomed to raise my arm against my countrymen, which I learnt too late was the purpose of Le Sage, whom I had taken for a captain of a merchantman, but found no other than commander of a kind of privateer. Fortune however, in this one instance, proved kinder to me than she had hitherto been accustomed, as, on this occasion, instead of falling in with some of the English merchantmen, as it was generally thought we should, and the ardent wish of Le Sage, our commander, we, after cruising about four months without any success, or meeting with anything worthy of notice, and then fell in with the British fleet, under the command of Admiral Lord Howe, then in the Channel.

On our first sight of the British, Le Sage ordered everyone to their duty; and observing me to be missing, he followed me to the place where I was concealed among the ballast, to which I had contrived to gain access through the cabin, in fear of being obliged to act against my country; and finding me persist in an obstinate refusal to come on deck, he beat me on the back and sides with a rope in a most inhuman manner, and drove me before him up the cabin stairs; but when on deck I absolutely refused to assist in defence of his vessel, and he being too much occupied to think only of me, left me to my own meditation. The British now bore down upon us, and, after a trifling resistance from the French, through desperation only, we were captured, and I considered as an English boy acting against my country, carried

15

with Le Sage and his companions before Lord Howe, on board the *Queen Charlotte*, to be examined.

Being interrogated by His Lordship respecting the cause of serving on board an enemy ship, I briefly told him:

That being without friends in England, I had accompanied a gentleman to the Continent in the capacity of foot-boy, on whose death, I had in the greatest distress reached Luxemburg, in hopes of obtaining a passage to my native country; but finding that impossible, it being at that time in possession of the French, I was constrained, though much against my inclination, to enter into Le Sage's vessel, having experienced during the short stay I made in the town, no attention to my distress, chiefly, as I imagined, from being English; and that my determination from the moment I engaged with Captain Le Sage was to desert the first opportunity that offered to forward my passage to England; but had I known the intention of Le Sage was to act in an offensive manner against my countrymen, I assured His Lordship, I would rather have perished than been induced to have set my foot on board his vessel; having, previous to sailing, taken him to be the commander of a merchantman, and as such engaged with him.

Fortunately, His Lordship did not think of questioning me concerning the place where my late master died; as in such an event I must unquestionably have acknowledged myself a deserter from the British forces at Valenciennes, being in no way prepared to resist such an enquiry; as my readers will be convinced that the whole of my answers to His Lordship's questions were founded on the hardships which I had experienced, and in no shape framed to deceive. This statement joined no doubt to the Frenchman's declaring my unwillingness to act in defence of the lugger, with the beating I had a little before experienced from Le Sage, gained me a favourable dismissal from Lord Howe, and served as a passport to a situation in one of the ships in His Lordship's fleet, on board of which I was immediately sent.

Elated with joy on beholding myself placed once more among my countrymen; as after my examination before Lord Howe, I was stationed on board the *Brunswick*, Captain John Hervey, where the story of my adventures, with the hardships I had suffered, gained me among the seamen as many friends as hearers, particularly for those I had undergone while on board the Frenchman. Our object in this cruise was to seek the fleet of the enemy, and bring on an engagement. The service allotted me, was to serve at the second gun on the quarter deck, and hand cartridge to the men; or, to speak in the seamen's phrase, to act in the capacity of *powder monkey*.

I had not however been long on board before Captain Hervey, observing my cleanliness, and manner different from many lads on board, called me to him, and questioned me as to my friends, and whether I had not run away from some school, to try the sea. Finding by my answers that I had been better brought up and educated than most in my present situation, he observed, if I would consider him as a confidential friend, and tell him the whole truth, I should find a protector in him, as he had children of his own, and could not tell what hardships they might encounter if he were dead. On which I told him I had neither father nor mother living, and that oppression from the person to whose care I was entrusted, had first caused my quitting home; and that in short, I was wholly destitute of any friend in the world. He appeared concerned at my early misfortunes in life, and promoted me immediately to be his principal cabin boy, in which capacity I continued to serve him until our fleet came within sight of the enemy.

Three months after my coming on board the *Brunswick*, our fleet fell in with that of the French, which brought on the ever memorable action of the 1st of June; an event which will ever be remembered with heartfelt satisfaction by the brave fellows who shared the toils of that auspicious day, and indeed by every lover of our glorious constitution and country. I cannot enter into a minute description of the action, being in the first part so busily engaged, and in the latter so much wounded; and shall, in consequence, commit a description of the part our gallant crew took in this exploit by what I afterwards was informed while lying under cure of the wounds I got while employed on board a ship, the glory of everyone who had the felicity of belonging to her, I mean the *Brunswick*.

This ship sustained a most tremendous conflict, being singly engaged for a considerable time with three seventy-fours. One of these she sent to the bottom; another, conceiving her much weakened from her exertions, determined to board, and manned her yards and shrouds, with a view of running up along-side, and flinging in all her crew at once. She observing this, with the greatest intrepidity and coolness, reserved a whole broadside, and in one discharge the *Brunswick* brought every mast by the board, and scattered her crew like so many mice upon the ocean. The other seventy-four yet remained, and now attempted to close with the *Brunswick*, harassed and enfeebled by her amazing efforts.

At this moment the *Ramillies*, commanded by Captain Hervey's brother, came up, and running in between the *Brunswick* and the Frenchman, took the enemy's fire, and relieved our gallant ship. So closely was she at times engaged, that she was unable to haul up her lower deck port lids, and was therefore obliged to fire through them. Nine were in consequence torn from her side; and the last broadside she gave, every muzzle of her lower deckers touched the copper of the enemy's bottom. The chief part of this action I was spectator as well as actor in, though strange to add, was not in the least intimidated. Just before the coming up of the *Ramillies*, I received a severe wound above the ankle of my left leg, by a grapeshot, that struck on the aftermost brace of the gun, which rebounding on the deck, lodged in my leg; notwithstanding which I attempted to rise three times, but without effect, and in the last effort part of the bone projected through the skin, in such a manner as wholly to prevent my standing, if I had been able to rise.

In addition to complete the misfortune, I received another wound by a musket-ball, that went completely through my thigh, a little above the knee of the same leg, and lay in this crippled state till the engagement was over; every person on board not wounded, being too much occupied to yield me the least assistance. I remained in this situation the rest of the action; but at length was conveyed, with many other wounded, to the cock-pit; where the surgeon, after making me suffer the most excruciating pain, could not extract the grape-shot from above my ankle, so completely was it lodged, and surrounded by the swelling which soon took place, and prevented his endeavour, through fear of injuring the tendons, among which he declared that it lay.

Our ship being so much shattered, it was deemed necessary she should be put in port to undergo repairs; in consequence of which we were towed into Spithead soon after the action: but the severity of my wounds obliged me to keep close to my birth, and was thus deprived of the gratifying pleasure of being hailed with those of my gallant messmates, who, on their arrival at Spithead, were greeted with the loudest acclamations of applause, by their grateful countrymen. With the first convenient opportunity, I was conveyed to Haslar hospital, at Gosport, and placed under the care of Surgeon Dodd, as outpatient, there not being sufficient room, from the number of wounded seamen, to admit me into the hospital: during this time I lay under his hands, I lodged at No. 2, Riemes Alley, Gosport, and supported myself with money I had received from Captain Hervey prior to the engagement. After four months attendance, and obtaining a partial cure; as Surgeon Dodd, though the utmost of his skill was exerted, could not extract the ball, it having lodged among the tendons, as before stated; to have cut among which, he said, would make me a cripple for life.

At length, little remaining but the scars which I shall carry to my grave, and having obtained in a great measure the use of my leg, I was discharged from the hospital, and soon after entered on board the *Vesuvius* bomb, Captain Tomlinson, then belonging to the squadron under the command of Sir Sydney Smith, lying at Spithead, and immediately commenced a cruise, in hopes of making prizes; but after some weeks cruising on the French coast without success, we steered for the Mediterranean, and, on our arrival at Gibraltar, came to an anchor, where we continued for three days. During that time we received an order to join the squadron under Sir Sydney Smith; on which we immediately weighed, and proceeded according to directions received.

Nothing worth notice occurred until we fell in with Sir Sydney and the ships under his command, in company of which we proceeded to Havre-de-Grace, where we were soon after separated in a gale; and continuing on the French coast with intent to rejoin Sir Sydney, fell in with two privateers near Dunkirk; from whom, observing their superior force, Captain Tomlinson endeavoured to make sail. The Frenchman observing his determination, crowded all the sail he could make, in chase; and we instantly commenced a running fire, which continued seven hours; at the end of which their superior weight of metal brought us to, and were in consequence immediately boarded. What became of Captain Tomlinson, the vessel, and part of the crew, I know not, as myself and William Richards, a young midshipman, (in which capacity I also acted on board the *Vesuvius*) were separated from the rest, and carried on board the other; but I have since reason to think the *Vesuvius* was recaptured, as she now continues in the British service.

When on board the privateer, who had taken us prisoners, we were deprived of our dirks, and conveyed to Dunkirk, where we were lodged in the prison of St. Clare, in Church-street, which had a little before belonged to the nuns of St. Clare, some of whom, since the revolution, have settled in England. Here I experienced the hardships of a French prison for the tedious space of eighteen months; in the course of which time Richards and myself projected a plan for our escape, by getting to the top of the prison, in order to jump off; but being observed by a sentinel on duty, we were both confined in separate dungeons, where it was so dark, that I never saw daylight, during the space of eleven weeks; and the only allowance I received, was bread and water, let down to me from the top of the cell. My bed consisted only of a little straw, not more than half a truss, which was never changed. For two days I was so ill in this dreadful place that I was unable to stir from my wretched bed of straw, to reach the miserable allowance; which, in consequence, was drawn up in the same state as it was the day before let down.

The next morning a person, who I suppose, was the keeper of the place, came into the dungeon without a light, (which way he came I know not, but suppose by a private door, through which I afterwards passed to be released) and called out to me, "Are you dead?" To this question I was only able to reply, by requesting a little water, being parched almost to death by thirst, resulting from the fever which preyed on me: he told me he had none, and left me in a brutal manner, without offering the least relief. Nature quickly restored me to health, and I sought the bread and water with as eager an inclination as a glutton would seek a feast. About five weeks after my illness, an exchange of prisoners taking place, I obtained my liberty, but did not see anything of Richards till after my arrival in England, where I met him by chance, near Covent-Garden.

During my residence in the prison of St. Clare, I observed among the rest of the prisoners, a very ingenious man, a German, who employed his time, and obtained more comforts in this place, than most others, by working gold wire in a particular manner, and which he disposed of, in the various shapes of bracelets, rings, and ornamental chains for ladies dresses. This man seemed fearful lest I should learn his method of workmanship, and was angry whenever I particularly noticed him at his work; notwithstanding, I contrived by frequent sight of the method he used, to bring the secret with me to England.

I was extremely weak, though in excellent spirits, on my deliverance from prison, but could scarcely bear the light for some days afterwards, it having an effect on my eyes, as if everything round me was chalk. I had thoughts of returning to England by the means of those who effected my release, but was diverted from this intention by the following circumstance:

Following my fellow prisoners just released, and from the pain in my leg, being considerably behind them, it was my chance to overhear the conversation of a gentleman making inquiries in English, of some seafaring men (by appearance) in Church-street, near the market, respecting any lad they knew, willing to make a voyage to America, in quality of ship's steward. I immediately accosted him, and proffered my service, being destitute of necessaries, and preferring such a situation, if I could obtain it, to a return to my native country, among the rest of my countrymen lately exchanged.

The gentleman immediately asked me my present situation at Dunkirk, which I briefly explained; in consequence of which I accompanied him back to the prison of St. Clare, where finding by the keepers of the prison that I had given him a true relation, he engaged me in the above capacity to perform the voyage to New-York, and from thence to England (which he informed me would be his next voyage) for 50*l.* and all I could make, at the same time advancing me sufficient cash in part, to fit me out.

His name was Captain John Field, of the *Ariel*, merchantman, New-York, on board which vessel I immediately embarked; and during our short stay at Dunkirk, was employed in correcting the ship's books, paying the men, victualling the ship, and taking in the cargo. Our vessel was chiefly laden with bale-goods, among which was French lace to the value of 5000*l.* We set sail for New-York, in the month of August 1796, and arrived after a successful and expeditious voyage of not more than a month, at the place of our destination, which, on going on shore I mistook for London, and particularly remarked a church, so like that in Covent-garden, that I was absolutely mistook it to be that church. I was detained little more than a fortnight at New-York, and was chiefly employed in taking an account of the goods delivered to the respective owners; after which duty I accepted an invitation to accompany my captain in an excursion to Providence State, in Rhode Island, where his family resided. During this journey, and indeed the whole of the voyage, I was considered rather as a friend and companion, by Captain Field, than a person in his pay, and under his command.

On our arrival at Rhode Island, we found Captain Field's family in good health; it consisted of his wife, four children and a niece. Here I spent the most agreeable fortnight of my life; as the captain neither paid not received any visits, but I made one of the party: Mrs. Field also appeared equally attached to me, which made the short time I continued among this worthy family, appear to me but as a dream, so few and transient were my days of happiness. Among other visits, we made one to Mr. Field, the captain's father, a very agreeable and worthy gentleman.

The only circumstance of an unpleasant nature that occurred during my stay in America, was the great partiality which the captain's niece had to my company, and which proceeded to such an extent, as to make me an offer of her hand in marriage.—I made several excuses, but could not divert her attention from what she proposed. Mrs. Field at length being acquainted with the circumstance, made my youth and inexperience in the world, a great objection; but neither my excuses, nor Mrs. Field's request had any weight, opposed to the young lady's inclination, which she endeavoured to accomplish to the last hour of my residence at Rhode Island. She requested before Mrs. Field, that I would make her a present of my picture; for which purpose I sat for a miniature at New-York, in the full uniform of an American officer—for this picture I paid eighteen dollars. The time of our departure for England being arrived, I reluctantly took my leave of Mrs. Field, and family; but had scarcely proceeded two miles on the way to New-York, before I was summoned back, being overtaken by a servant, who informed the captain and myself, that we must come back, as the young lady was in strong fits. We returned, and found her still in a fit, out of which, with great difficulty, we recovered her; and I by making her a promise of a speedy return from England, with great reluctance on her part, took my final departure.

Our stay at New-York was but short; the mate, in the absence of Captain Field and myself, having taken charge of the cargo consigned to England, and obtained the necessary invoices of the goods; chiefly manufactured cotton and camblets. This, had I remained on board, would have been part of my duty; but through the indulgence of the captain, it was performed by another. We proceeded on our voyage to England with a favourable wind, and arrived at Cowes, in the Isle of Wight, without meeting with anything particular on the way. Our provisions falling short, we took in some fresh, and after waiting three days for a convoy, proceeded to the River Thames, where we safely cast anchor on the 20th of November, 1796, and came to a mooring in the tier off Church-hole, Rotherhithe.

We delivered our cargo, and had been some days taking in a fresh one, Captain Field not thinking of staying longer in England than absolutely necessary for taking in an outward bound cargo. The many acts of friendship which I had experienced from this gentleman, determined me to accompany him in any voyage he might undertake; particularly as he had often informed me that if I continued with him a voyage or two more, he would resign the command of the vessel to me; it being his intention to retire from the sea service in a short time. He told me that he had an idea of making a trading voyage up the Mediterranean, and commissioned me to purchase some maps, charts, &c. necessary for such an undertaking, which I in consequence bought (at Faden's, who then resided at the corner of St. Martin's Lane, Strand,) by his direction.

Being short of men to work the ship, the captain had engaged two fresh hands, who came on board the afternoon of the same day, myself being the only officer on board; I took the description of their persons, and entered their names on the ship's books, being employed at the same time in settling my accounts in the cabin, and having some loose cash, and banknotes lying on the desk. After giving them orders to assist in swabbing the decks the first thing in the morning, I dismissed them.

Soon after twelve o'clock at night, I was awakened by a violent noise at the upper cabin door, with a crash, as if some part of it had given way. Alarmed at the moment, I searched for a tinder-box, to strike a light, but through hurry could not lay my hand on it, almost at the same instant I caught hold of a brace of pistols, which hung on the side of the cabin fireplace; these, to my great surprise, I found unloaded. A second attempt of a more violent nature than the first, being made at the inner door, I recollected a sword which hung over the captain's berth, and which I took down; at the instant the cabin door had given way, by a wrench from an iron crow, or some such instrument. I knowing the situation of the door, with the sword in my hand made towards it, and immediately made a thrust that I knew must wound deep, from the difficulty I found in drawing it back.

I heard neither groan, or noise; but found that the intruder, whoever he was, retired. I now sought the tinder-box, and struck a light, secured the door, and sat up the remainder of the night. The first thing in the morning the men observed a quantity of blood on the deck, in a track from the cabin door, which they noticed as being broke, and asked me if anything particular had happened; to which I made no reply; but on finding MacGregory, one of the new engaged hands, to be absent, I inquired after him, and was informed that he was unwell from an accident he had met with the night before in getting into his berth. I made no other inquiries; but waited until the captain should come on board, which he did about eleven o'clock the same morning; and on entering the cabin, he noticed the shattered condition of the door.

When I informed him of the particulars, adding, that the man whom I suspected, MacGregory, still remained in the ship; the captain instantly ordered him to be brought forward, when his thigh was discovered to be dreadfully swelled, and the marks of the wound shewed a sword or some such weapon to have passed through his thigh. He could make no defence to my accusation of his attempt to rob the cabin, and breaking the door. Captain Field finding his wound dangerous, sent him to St. Thomas's hospital, where he escaped prosecution, by the ship's sailing before he could obtain a cure.

A few days after this affair, the mate, John Jones, (a native of New-Providence) and myself, agreed on a little excursion on shore, previous to our leaving England, to which purpose we put on a plain seaman's dress, knowing the prejudice of most of the lower people about Wapping, against officers of any description, whom in general they consider as little better than spies on their actions. But while about to land at St. Catherine's, we were attacked by a press-gang, whom we resolutely opposed; I in my defence taking up one of the skullers of the boat, with which I struck one or two who attempted to secure me. In this contest I received a wound on my head by a cutlass, a large seam from which remains to the present hour.

After a long struggle, during which I was tumbled out of the boat up to my armpits in water, the mate and myself were both secured. Fortunately for him, he had his warrant as an American officer about him, which procured his discharge, when taken on board the tender. On my examination, being unprepared for such an event, I had inadvertently left my protection as an American on board the *Ariel*, behind me. This circumstance, with the treachery of Jones, who informed the regulating captain that I was an Englishman, thereby thinking to get rid of a dangerous rival, (for he was particularly attached to the niece of Captain Field, but had lost all hope of success with her, from her known partiality for me) and moreover stated I was the best seaman on board their vessel.

This declaration, joined with the want of the certificate I had left in the *Ariel*, occasioned my detention on board the tender for three days and nights. In this situation my indignation at the treachery of Jones, agitated me beyond anything I had hitherto suffered; and I thought of various schemes, but without putting any in practice, to effect my deliverance. At length there being a sufficient number of impressed men collected to clear the tender for the reception of others, myself and the rest of the men confined were brought upon deck, in order to be sent to different ships. Finding I had nothing to prevent this, but a disclosure of what I had so long kept within my own breast, I accosted the inspecting officers, and told them I was unfit to serve His Majesty in the way of my fellow-sufferers, being a female. On this assertion they both appeared greatly surprised; and at first thought I had fabricated a story to be discharged, and sent me to the surgeon, whom I soon convinced of the truth of my assertion. The officers upbraided each other with ignorance at not discovering before, that I was a woman, and readily gave me a discharge.

Resolved never to go on board the *Ariel*, after the disclosure of my sex, I wrote to Captain Field, without mentioning the way in which I obtained a discharge from the tender, only requesting he would meet me as soon as possible at a house at the corner of Tower Street, Tower Hill. He being on board at the time, my letter had not been dispatched long, before he gave me the meeting, and was astonished, at my disclosing to him the manner in which I obtained my liberty.

It was some time before I could convince him that I was really a woman; having for such a length of time known me experience hardships so opposite to the delicacy of the female sex. He endeavoured to prevail on me to accompany him in his intended voyage, but no arguments could induce me (after acknowledging former favours received) to accompany him, nor indeed for the present to think of the sea-service, in any way whatever. Finding his applications fruitless, he honourably paid me every shilling due on our engagement, and beside made me a very handsome present. After this interview I saw him but twice, nothing material passing between us, except his earnest desire of my disguising my sex, and resuming my former situation, which he could never prevail on me to accede to.

With money in my pocket, I was undetermined how to act, but for the present took a lodging in East-Smithfield, and during my residence here, made several applications at the Navy Pay Office, Somerset House, for money due to me for service on board the Brunswick, and the Vesuvius bomb, from which I was taken by the French, exclusive of prize-money I was entitled to, by captures on the first of June. At length I was directed to apply respecting the prize-money to the Agent, No. 4, Arundell-street, Strand, where I immediately went, and was desired to call another time; being vexed at the disappointment, I returned to Somerset House; where through many disappointments, I made use of language which gave offence to some of the gentlemen, and was immediately conveyed to Bow-street, on the 31st of December, 1796.

Here I underwent a long examination, which lasted till near twelve o'clock, before the sitting magistrate, now Sir Richard Ford, to whom I produced my discharge from the tender, and other documents to prove the sufferings and hardships which I had undergone, so much to his satisfaction, that I obtained a discharge, and was requested to attend the Monday following at two o'clock, which I did, and found several magistrates assembled, where I underwent a long private examination, the consequence was, a subscription was immediately made, and by the recommendation of some gentlemen present, I was placed in a lodging at the house of Mrs. Jones, Falcon Court, Shoe-lane, with a strict injunction, if possible, to break me of the masculine habit to which I was so much used. I received twelve shillings a week for a support till I could get the money due to me from government. The above sum was regularly paid me from the above subscription, by a Mr. Pritchard of New-Inn, who was present at my last examination, and to whom Mrs. Jones was laundress.

I had not yet changed my seaman's attire; but during the stay I made with Mrs. Jones, I resumed the dress of my own sex, though at times I could not so far forget my seafaring habits, but frequently dressed myself, and took excursions as a sailor. In less than a month, I received the greater part of the money due to me from the Navy Pay Office, which I cheerfully participated in the family of Mrs. Jones; who, notwithstanding, treated me in an ungrateful manner, misrepresenting me to the gentlemen who had raised the subscription, as a person on whom their bounty was misplaced, and being inclined to masculine propensities, more than what became a female, such as smoking, drinking grog, &c. though I never took any of the latter, but she was always invited to a part, and of which I never found her backward in taking a good allowance. Whenever I dressed myself as a sailor, I sought the company of some messmates I had known on board the *Brunswick*, and as long as my money lasted, spent it in company with the brave fellows, at the Coach and Horses, opposite Somerset-House, a place where they mostly frequented.

I removed from Mrs. Jones's to Chichester Rents, Chancery-lane, and lodged with a very decent woman, named Higgins, where the grape-shot which had remained in my leg from the time of our engagement in the Brunswick, June 1794, worked itself out in February 1797—the reason I imagine, proceeded from the wounds breaking out afresh, in consequence of my too free use of spirituous liquors, since my residence on shore. I kept the ball, by me for some time, to which there adhered a quantity of flesh; but was obliged at last to throw it in the fire, from the offensive smell of the flesh, which soon putrefied. My leg, notwithstanding the ball was out, continued so bad, that I applied for admission to St. Bartholomew's hospital, and went in as a female, though I frequently wore, while under cure, my sailor's dress, and in consequence was taken as a man in the woman's ward, by strangers.

I remained in Watt's ward, under Surgeon Blake four months, and during the time had several pieces of shattered bone taken from my leg; and at length it being to all appearance well, I was discharged. The cure, however, did not prove of any long duration, the bone being very much injured, and my blood continuing in a bad state, it soon broke out again. In this situation, without any place of refuge, or means of subsistence, I was advised to petition His Royal Highness the Duke of York for relief; and accordingly applied to a gentleman, who drew up a petition, stating the various hardships I had undergone by sea and land and got it signed by Her Grace the Duchess of Devonshire, and Sir William Pulteney, I left it at the Horse Guards, with Captain Nowell, secretary to His Royal Highness. In less than a fortnight, I called at the Horse Guards, and received from Captain Nowell five guineas, with my petition signed by His Royal Highness, as well as Her Royal Highness the Duchess of York, and directions, when I called, that I should present it to Her Majesty.

I afterwards got it signed by Sir James Pulteney; and through Mr. Dundas, meant to have presented it to Her Majesty; I taking the opportunity of a court day to give it to him for that purpose, as he was passing to the royal apartments. He remarked it was not intended for him, I told him no—but I wished him to present it to Her Majesty from myself, and accordingly left it with him.

Not hearing anything in consequence of my petition, and the money I had received from His Royal Highness the Duke of York, being expended, I, for my present support, thought if I could obtain a machine similar to the one I observed the German use in the prison of St. Clare, with which he manufactured the gold wire, I might obtain a comfortable subsistence. For that purpose I called on Mr. Loyer, a jeweller, in Denmark-street, St. Giles's, in order, if possible, to get a machine made from my description. Mr. Loyer, from my instructions, soon produced an instrument that every way answered the purpose; and having informed him of the use for which it was intended, he informed me, if I would manufacture it in his house, he had no doubt he could from his connection, dispose of enough to keep me constantly employed.

I made no objection to his proposal, and worked gold wire in various shapes, so much to his satisfaction, that I continued in his employ some time. Mr. Loyer keeping a number of persons employed, myself, as well as others, worked together; among whom was a German, named Hieronimo, who, observing the manner in which I worked, afterwards practised it as part of his profession, and worked on the same, during the time I continued in Mr. Loyer's employ. Finding the money received not adequate to support me in a proper manner, my wounded leg getting so bad as to put me to considerable inconvenience, I applied to Mr. Loyer for an advancement of price, which, he objecting to, knowing that he had Hieronimo to work it if I left him, we parted. Before which, being jealous I should learn everything in the jewellery business, having been able to work in more branches than the one he engaged me for, he removed me for some time previous to my quitting him, to a separate apartment from the shop, where I worked by myself.

On my quitting Mr. Loyer's, my leg getting worse, I obtained admission into St. George's hospital, and experienced a tedious confinement of seven months, being carefully attended by Surgeons Keate and Griffiths; and while thus situated, was enabled to enjoy many comforts which this charitable institution does not supply, from the benevolent attention of Mrs. Emma Raynes, a lady to whom I shall ever confess my obligations, as, immediately on my obtaining a discharge from the hospital, she provided me with a decent lodging in Tottenham Court Road, and supported me for a considerable time at her own expense, though I had no other claim to her protection than my necessitous condition.

Previous to my finding a friend in this lady, it was judged by several in the hospital, from the low state I was reduced to, (my bones coming almost through the skin) that I should not get over the illness under which I laboured, from the pain of my wounded limb, and I procured some little necessaries from a subscription made by the young gentlemen, pupils, who attended the hospital; one of whom, named Saife, (I imagine) in joke, offered me half-a-crown a week while I lived, to have my body when dead. However he might mean it, I knew not, but this circumstance produced in me such an aversion to physic, that while I remained under cure, I would take no more medicine, fearing it would hasten my death; and I remarked that my wound healed faster than before. Weary of the hospital, I solicited a discharge, though my leg was by no means well; and through the kindness of Mrs. Raynes, had every necessary provided for my use.

Unwilling to remain a burthen on the generosity of this lady, longer than I could possibly help myself, I came to a resolution of making my sufferings known to some persons of distinction, (having heard nothing relative to the petition I had left in the hands of Mr. Dundas, to be presented to Her Majesty). I wrote immediately to His Grace the Duke of Norfolk, whose humane and charitable disposition is so well known, for me to enlarge on. The result of my application was successful, as I received a very handsome present from His Grace, to whom I was introduced, after waiting some time in his library.

This seasonable relief was to me of the greatest service, though it contributed to place me under a very embarrassing circumstance. Fearing that my little fund would be exhausted before I could obtain another supply, I endeavoured, as far as my circumstances would admit, to make as decent an appearance as possible, that I might more readily appear before the illustrious personages who had recommended the presentation of my petition to Her Majesty, and to obtain, if possible, a knowledge, whether it had been presented by Mr. Dundas, or not. At this time I had removed from the lodging provided me by Mrs. Raynes to another near Rathbone Place; and having at times, previous to my removal, wore a little powder in my hair whenever I had occasion to call at the houses of noble persons, to whom I had made my case known, I was informed against as an unqualified person, having no licence, through the malice of my last landlady's sister, and received a summons to attend the Commissioners of the Stamp Office, from the solicitor, Mr. Estcourt, in February 1799,—to answer to the accusation.

Under this situation, without money or a friend to come forward on my behalf, I attended on the day mentioned in the notice which I had received, and set up in my defence to the accusation, that I had never worn powder as an article of dress though I had frequently made use of it in defence of my king and country. This assertion from a female excited the curiosity of the commissioners; who questioned me, under what circumstance, I could make use of powder in the way understood from my speech; when I related the several incidents of my life, in the land, as well as sea service, likewise my examination at Bow Street, after applying for my pay at the Navy Office.

On concluding my defence, and remarking the distress of my present situation, the commissioners, and other gentlemen present made a handsome collection, and presented me with it to the extreme mortification of the informer, who rather expected a share of the penalty, which she supposed I should be under the necessity of paying, than, that her spite against me should turn out so much to my advantage. On the contrary, my late landlady, her sister, expressed herself greatly pleased with the fortunate turn in my favour; and her sincerity I did not doubt, from the many little kindnesses I had before experienced from her. Mr. Estcourt, the gentleman from whom I received the notice to attend on the commissioners, gave me a letter to Evan Nepean, Esq. of the Admiralty, on what subject I knew not, but rather suppose to be in relation to myself; which, though I delivered at the Admiralty office, I never heard anything of after.

To avoid as much as possible future disagreeable, and to obtain a sum which might enable me to establish myself in a little comfort, I thought on the petition I had long since left in the hands of Mr. Dundas; and as it was originally recommended to be presented to Her Majesty, by the message I had received from His Royal Highness the Duke of York, I resolved to wait on His Royal Highness at Oatlands, to inform him that I had never received an answer to his royal recommendation. On my arrival at Oatlands, I sent in my name and business, by one of the attendants on His Royal Highness—and received in answer a guinea, and a message that His Royal Highness would make an immediate enquiry concerning where the petition lay; and as I had left a direction where I lodged in town, a few days after I received a quantity of female apparel from Oatlands—sent, as I imagine, by order of Her Royal Highness the Duchess of York.

The long silence which I have kept with regard to Mr. Sucker, particularly as he was the only person, who could have informed me of many circumstances relative to my family and interests, I need not offer as an excuse for my negligence in this particular that:

> I had been so much occupied by a variety of circumstances, each following the other with a rapidity as wholly to prevent, had it been my intention, an earlier seeking his explanation.

> I had in a great measure been prevented applying to Mr. Suck-

er before, in consequence of Messrs. Winter and Hay, of Long Acre, through the recommendation of Justice Bond, having taken the trouble of writing to Mr. Wilson of Trevallyn several times, for the particulars relating to my birth and expectations; but as he never obtained an answer to either of the letters sent, I thought it best to apply to Mr. Sucker in person. During the doubt I remained under with respect to the success of my petition, I determined to pay this gentleman a visit, and went to Shrewsbury, by the mail; and put up at the Talbot, kept at that time by Mr. Purslow.

I then proceeded to Newport, Mr. Sucker's residence, in a return post chaise; but finding a difficulty of being introduced to him as a female, not chusing to send in my name, but that a lady wished to speak with him, which not succeeding to my expectation, I returned to Shrewsbury, and procured an ensign's uniform of a person in Dog Lane, who dealt in clothes from London. Not wishing to change my dress at Mr. Purslow's, where I was known, I went to the Raven Inn, in Raven Street, where I changed my female attire, for the one I had procured the loan of—in which dress I walked to the Elephant and Castle, in Mardol, and hiring a horse, rode back to Newport.

When I called at Mr. Sucker's house, I sent a message in by a servant, that a gentleman wished to speak with Mr. Sucker, and in return received an answer to send in my name and business; to which I replied, I waited on him, having known Captain Bowen of the 82nd regiment, and had something particular to communicate; on which I was immediately introduced to him, and though labouring under considerable agitation, I asked him if he knew a Miss Talbot, or could inform me what had become of her. He said he had known her well, but that she had died abroad in the year 1793, of which he was well informed by letters in his possession. I told him I doubted the fact, and wished to see the letters mentioned, which he evaded.

I then asked him if she had any particular mark, or that he should know her well enough to swear to her person, if he was to see her. He replied that he could identify her, among a thousand, that she was a twin, and had a deficiency on the left side of her forehead, I immediately put my hair aside, and pointed my finger, to the part of my forehead he had described, and briskly drawing my sword, declared he was my prisoner, and should account to me for the deficiency of what I supposed he had defrauded me.

I informed him that I was Miss Talbot, and had visited him, for the express purpose of obtaining the property he had certainly deprived me of, knowing, that when I was entrusted to his care, he had a sufficient indemnification for what trouble or expense he might be put to, and had no doubt something considerable in trust for my use. He appeared surprised and confounded, and uttering he was a ruined man repeatedly, he trembled much, and abruptly quitted the room. I was myself greatly agitated, but conceiving myself so much injured, I immediately went to Shrewsbury, in order to take a lawyer's advice how I should proceed, and applied to a Mr. Locksdale, who unfortunately was from home, getting no satisfactory intelligence, I returned to Newport with a determination, if possible, to get from Mr. Sucker, an information of my family, connections, and expectations.

When I arrived at Newport, I learnt to my great disappointment, that Mr. Sucker had suddenly retired from his house, and in less than three days from the time, was found dead in his bed at a place called Longford, near Newport, without any previous appearance of illness. Thus frustrated in gaining the intelligence I so much needed, I left the place in great distress of mind, with a scanty pittance in my pocket, which wholly prevented from proceeding to Mr. Wilson's at Trevallyn, which I otherwise should have done, though his wilful neglect in answering the letters sent by Messrs. Winter and Hay, left me in great doubt as to the reception he might have given me. I now took the road to London, where I soon arrived without any other prospect than the uncertain hope of better success with my petition, and thinking some money was still due to me for pay, I applied to Lord Spencer, then First Lord of the Admiralty, and saw His Lordship, who presented me with a guinea, and ordered me some refreshment; when I had an excellent breakfast prepared in an adjoining room.

My existence now chiefly depended on the liberality of many noble and generous persons, to whom I was necessitated to make my case known; and the frequent walks I was obliged to take in the course of the days I was so employed, caused the wounds of my leg to break out again, as wholly to deprive me of the power of walking, many pieces of the shattered bone occasionally coming out of my leg. To remedy this, I got admitted into Middlesex hospital, and about a fortnight after my admission, I received a message from Justice Bond, to attend if possible at Bow Street, to confront a female, who, in the dress of a Light Horseman, had taken the name of John Taylor, and represented herself in a way to be mistaken for me.

I accompanied the person who brought me the letter to Bow Street, and saw a fine looking woman about five feet ten inches high, whom Mr. Bond desired me to question as to the situation she had occupied on board the *Brunswick*, where she reported herself to have been wounded.

A very few questions brought her to a confession, that she was not the person she had pretended, and not giving a satisfactory account of herself, she was committed to the House of Correction for three months, as a vagrant. William Richards, my fellow prisoner in France, chancing to pass in Bow Street, I called to him from the coach, and he went in with me into the office and offered to make oath as to my identity; but Mr. Bond informed him that he was sufficiently satisfied who was the impostor. Several persons in the office informed me that this woman had been imposing on the public in my name for some time past, and congratulated me on her detection.

On my return from Bow Street, while getting out of the coach at the door of my lodging where I called previous to my return to the hospital, I was followed into the passage by a hair-dresser, named Spraggs, of Cleveland Street, who mistaking me for a lodger in the same house with whom he had a dispute respecting a wig which she had of him, struck me a violent blow which brought me to the ground, and cut my head in a shocking manner, and materially hurt my wounded leg by kicking me in the passage. I afterwards learnt that the cause of his violence was as follows: that he had sold a wig to a lady, and she was prevented paying him, by the assertion of another hairdresser, that the wig was not his property to sell, but belonged to him, a Mr. Kennedy.

Mr. Spraggs in consequence, when he applied for payment, learnt the particulars; and not getting the money he expected, brought an action in the Marshalsea Court, but was nonsuited, by not attending to prove the wig his property. Thus disappointed, he took the above method of revenge, and in rage mistook the person; my friends advised me to get a warrant for the assault, and I immediately returned to Bow Street, where a warrant was granted me. Spraggs, however, kept out of the way for several days, but at last it was served on him, and he was obliged to find bail for his appearance at the Quarter Sessions, Clerkenwell Green;—by returning to Bow Street, on the day I left the hospital, I could not return there that night, and was obliged to wait till the regular day of taking in patients, before I could regain my former place in the hospital.

When the trial came on at Clerkenwell, I was still in the hospital, but knowing the time it was to come on, I requested leave of absence from Surgeon Miners, which I obtained and attended three days before my cause came on. Mr. Sylvester, the present Recorder of London, pleaded my cause, without taking the least gratuity; on the contrary, when I attended him to state to him the case, he made me a handsome present. Very little defence was attempted on the part of Spraggs, who was found guilty of the assault, and sentenced to pay me 10l. for the injury he had done. The trial over I returned to Middlesex Hospital, and through the skill and attention of Surgeon Miners, I was once more enabled to use my wounded leg, though by no means given to understand that I had obtained a radical cure.

Soon after quitting the hospital, I received a notice to attend at the War Office, where I received a letter directed to Lord Morton, at Buckingham House. Struck at once that it related to the petition I had left for Her Majesty's sight, and which I imagined His Royal Highness the Duke of York had sought after, agreeable to the message I received at Oatlands. I went to Buckingham House, and saying I had a letter from the War Office for Lord Morton, was immediately introduced to His Lordship, who, on reading the letter, informed me that it related to my petition, and conducted me to another apartment, where I saw a lady seated, whose hand Lord Morton desired me to kiss; after which, I returned with His Lordship to the apartment I was first introduced to, and received five guineas from His Lordship's hands, on quitting Buckingham House.

The lady whose hand I kissed did not ask me a question, nor speak a word: I imagined it might be Her Majesty, though Lord Morton had not mentioned anything concerning her title or rank. But I was soon after confirmed in my opinion by recognising in the sight of Her Majesty in public, the lady whose hand I had the honour of kissing at Buckingham House. Lord Morton directed me to apply to the War Office, where I was informed I must attend on a future day, in my sailor's dress, to receive a half-year's payment of Her Majesty's bounty, which I afterwards did, in the name of John Taylor, though my name on the War-office book stood Taylor, John. This was in August, 1799.

On my quitting Middlesex Hospital, Surgeon Miners informed me, my leg was not in a state to bear much walking, and the obligation I was under to attend in person, on many occasions, brought on the complaint in my leg as bad as ever. I was recommended by John Bond, Esq. a magistrate, of Hendon, in Middlesex, to go into Middlesex Hospital a second time. Surgeon Miners was at Mr. Bond's at the time I was thus advised, and told me that I must in all probability have my leg amputated. With this impression on my mind I entered the hospital a second time, and only escaped from thence without the loss of a limb, by a singular, though in the first part, unfortunate circumstance:—I had, previous to going into the hospital, taken under my care a motherless child about three years of age, which when out of my power now to attend, was protected by two young ladies, who soon after having an engagement to dine on board the *Sophia*, a West-Indiaman, lying off Hermitage Stairs, unfortunately took their little charge on the party, who not being sufficiently attended to, fell overboard and was drowned.

The intelligence no sooner reached me at the hospital, then frantic at the loss of the child, although my leg was surrounded with bandages in order for amputation, I the next morning by seven o'clock, October 24th, 1799, quitted the hospital, after taking off the screw bandage, and walked to Hermitage Stairs, in such distraction of mind, that I felt neither pain nor impediment in my leg the whole way. But on my arrival where the ship lay, I could gain no information concerning the body, and though I offered everything I had in the world as a reward to find it.—but without effect, as the child was never after seen; it was afterwards suggested, and on reasonable grounds, that the child was not drowned, but carried to the West Indies; as a black boy on board, as well as he could be understood, gave me to understand, the child was not drowned, but carried away. His name was George Lacon Griffin, and heir to a considerable estate in Shropshire, as I was informed by his father, Mr. George Griffin, a carver and gilder, burnt out in February, 1804, at No. 16, Charing Cross, who entrusted me with the care of the child; being himself under a pecuniary embarrassment, and in confinement at that time, by a bill he had accepted for a friend.

A few days after my leaving Middlesex Hospital a second time, the following paragraph appeared in the *Morning Herald* of November 1st, 1799:—

There is at present in the Middlesex Hospital, a young and delicate female, who calls herself Miss T-lb-t, and who is said to be related to some families of distinction; her story is very singular; at an early period of her life, having been deprived, through the villainy of a trustee, of a sum of money bequeathed by her deceased relation of high rank, she followed the fortunes of a young naval officer to whom she was attached, and personated a common sailor before the mast: during a lover's quarrel, she quitted her ship, and assumed for a time the military character; but her passion for the sea prevailing, she returned to her favourite element, and did good service, and receiving a severe wound on board Earl St. Vincent's ship, on the glorious 14th of February; and again bled in the cause of her country, in the engagement off Camperdown; on this occasion her knee was so shattered, that an amputation is likely to ensue. This spirited female, we understand, receives 20*l.* from an illustrious lady, which is about to be doubled.

By whom this paragraph was inserted in the paper, I know not; but the readers will easily discover it could be no person who really knew my story, having quitted Middlesex Hospital some time before; the only part that resembles truth, is of Her Majesty's Bounty, which had not yet reached me: though in that particular the writer has been pleased to announce what I should be happy to receive.

I had not left Middlesex Hospital more than a fortnight, before I experienced new trouble and inconvenience in my leg; which, previous to my so sudden departure, on the melancholy loss of the unfortunate child, had been doomed to amputation, by the universal opinion of the surgeons; and to the general conversation on this subject, I attribute a spurious account of my adventures, which at this time found its way into the *Morning Herald.* As I did not wait for a discharge from Middlesex Hospital, I felt a reluctance to apply there again for relief, but obtained an order to the St. Mary-le-bone Infirmary, where I obtained an order, and was of course admitted. Here I continued almost four months; and after many pieces of the shattered bone had been extracted, and the flesh by continued rest, a little grown over, I consulted with Mr. Phillips, the principal surgeon, whether I was not in a situation to quit the infirmary. He told me that with care, and the use of bandages he would give me, I might do as well out as where I was, but desired I would walk as little as possible, while I found the least pain, as it would retard the healing of the flesh round the bone.

Having obtained the bandages of Mr. Waller, the house surgeon, I immediately thought of quitting the infirmary, but having made myself useful towards the latter part of the time I was there, in keeping account of clothes, and marking a variety of articles, for the use of the infirmary and parish, Dr. Hooper, the principal of the house, objected to my departure, which notwithstanding I insisted on, and in consequence came away; as Doctor Hooper said he would report me to the Board, I told him I would save him the trouble, and went the following Friday, and stated the whole affair myself, which being satisfactory to the gentlemen present, I received two guineas, and well pleased left the place. One of the gentlemen said, he knew Mrs. Tapperley, of Chester well, and that he had a daughter under her care, during the time I was with her, adding, that he knew I was related to the family whose name I bore, and following me out, made me a present of a guinea; and I have since, whenever he met me, experienced some mark of his liberality.

Having engaged a lodging in that neighbourhood, I removed the whole of my wearing apparel, which in all situations I had hitherto taken the utmost care of, to this place. But as if I was to be stripped and persecuted through life, one morning while in bed, I was robbed of everything I possessed in the world, and but for the kindness of some ladies at the next house, should have been without an article to wear. A woman who lived with a trumpeter of the Dragoon Guards, was soon afterwards taken up on suspicion of robbing another person, and having in her possession a great quantity of false keys, and duplicates of property in pawn; I attended her examination at Marlborough-street, and discovered that several of the duplicates to describe my property! I was desired to attend on her trial, as a witness; though in applying to the pawnbrokers, where she had pledged them, I was informed the same was taken away by an affidavit of the loss of the duplicates. She was, however, found guilty of the robbery taken up for, and sentenced to be transported for seven years.

A little time after this affair, I received a half year's payment of Her Majesty's bounty, and not forgetting my former frolics, of which I was not yet entirely cured, I went out in company of a person I knew in male attire; after walking some time, it was proposed to take a tankard of porter, and we went into a public house the corner of Beswick Street, Oxford Road; while drinking, I was accosted by a recruiting sergeant of the 21st regiment of Light Dragoons, whose name I understood was Jones, who thinking from my appearance and conversation, I was a fit subject for his purpose, used every endeavour, by praising the life of a horse soldier, of inveigling me to enlist. Finding the attempt fruitless, and doubting to effect it by persuasion, he had recourse to artifice, and proposed tossing with me for a pot of porter, taking a guinea from his pocket and tossing it on the table, thinking I might take it up.

But perceiving the drift of his intention, I gave him to understand,

I was not so easily to be taken in. My friend also joining me, a dispute was likely to ensue, but instantly leaving the house, he followed us the distance of several streets, and seemed reluctantly to give up the pursuit.

Many professions struck my imagination to take up as a livelihood, but none appeared more congenial to my mind than the theatrical line, to which I was ever particularly attached. Knowing a person belonging to the Thespian Society, held in Tottenham-court-road, I got introduced to perform a character, and attempted that of Floranthe, in the *Mountaineers*, which I got through with considerable applause. Mr. Talbot, afterwards of Drury-lane Theatre, performed the part of Octavian, and Miss Mortimer of Covent-garden, played Agnes. I afterwards performed the parts of Adeline, in the *Battle of Hexham*; Lady Helen, in the *Children in the Wood*; Juliet, in *Romeo and Juliet*; Irene, in *Barbarossa*; Thyra, in *Athelstan*; the Queen, in *Richard the Third*; Mrs. Scout in the *Village Lawyer*, and Jack Hawser in *Banyan Day*. Finding this pursuit, however, more pleasant than profitable, I was compelled to give it up, and solicit assistance towards my support, from several respectable persons to whom I had made my adventures and sufferings known.

A remarkable circumstance which I cannot by any means omit, as it had nearly involved me in a situation, more dangerous than any to which I had hitherto encountered. About the time my adventures attracted the attention of the first characters in the kingdom, I received several sums of money from persons, who at the time, did not discover to whom I was obliged, and one evening a gentleman called at my lodgings, and on being introduced to my apartments, asked me if I was the person who had suffered so many hardships abroad. I replied in the affirmative; when he informed me Colonel Gerrit Fisher, of the 9th regiment of Foot, had been particularly inquiring concerning me, and he had no doubt it would produce something considerable to my advantage. He shortly took his leave, and about a month after, called in my absence, and left with Mrs. Cornish, who kept a shop at No. 14, Suffolk-street, at which house I lodged, an order signed by Colonel Fisher, on Messrs. Cox and Co. Craig's Court, Charing Cross, for nine guineas, saying at the same time, it was the amount of money received in subscription for my use, by Colonel Fisher.

He also left a complimentary note, in which he styled himself Captain Grant, and was accompanied by a person who was introduced to me as a servant of Colonel Fisher's, and confirmed what Grant said.

This order came as I then thought, providentially to my aid, but it being holiday time, I waited a few days, after which, in company with Mrs. Cornish, I presented it for payment as directed, but was informed that Colonel Fisher was out of town, and they could not pay it. Very much disappointed, I returned home, and as I did not hear when the colonel was expected in town, it was a considerable time after that I thought of calling on him respecting the transaction, which at length I did, at his house, No. 5, Manchester Square, February 2nd, 1802.

On saying that I wished to speak with Colonel Fisher on business, he came into the passage, and understanding in part what I had to say, introduced me into the parlour, where I saw a lady seated, who I afterwards found was the colonel's lady. I now presented him with the note, and asked him if it was his handwriting. On reading it over, he asked me how I came by it, and when I told him it was left at my apartments by a gentleman, who said it was the amount of what Colonel Fisher had raised in subscription for me; the colonel requested a description of the gentleman's person, and gave me pen and ink to write it down, on which I first described the gentleman who had called, and reported Colonel Fisher's interesting himself on my account, and was about to write the particulars down, when Mrs. Fisher prevented me, by saying to the colonel, "It surely must be Gardiner."

To which he made no reply, but putting the order into his waistcoat pocket, said he would take care of it, though he did not give me a shilling. A few days afterwards, he called at my lodgings, and seeing Mrs. Cornish, asked her who, and what I was, and whether she did not think I had forged the order? Mrs. Cornish then related the same particulars of my possessing the order, as I had before informed him. He then left the house, telling Mrs. Cornish if she had not given a good account of the way the draft was left, he should have prosecuted us both for a forgery.—I afterwards called at his house, and sending up my name, was told by a servant, my business required no answer, since when, I have never heard anything of him or his order.

Whether or not the order was of Colonel Fisher's handwriting, or a trick played on me by the man who styled himself Captain Grant, I never could learn, but as the clerks of Cox and Co. must have been acquainted with the handwriting of the colonel, and never attempted to stop it, or say it was a forgery, I cannot bring myself to think it was so. Nor did the colonel himself say to me it was not his writing, only questioned how I came by it.

With the certainty of my income from Her Majesty's bounty, I removed to the neighbourhood of Whitechapel, some time previous to my waiting on Colonel Fisher; and having been ever more remiss in my own accounts than those of others, the landlady where I had taken my abode, brought me in a bill for lodging, &c. amounting to 11*l*. 3*s*. 6*d*. which being incapable of paying, I was arrested at her suit in the court of Exchequer. And after remaining at a lock-up house, in Carey-street, Lincoln's-Inn-Fields, a week, and being sufficiently tired of the expense, I was removed to Newgate, though not before I had been enabled by a friend to offer down six guineas in part of the debt, which was rejected. A new scene in life now opened to my view, and finding many of my fellow prisoners of a congenial temper with my own, I frequently joined in parties of conviviality hardly to be credited in this place. These pleasures, however, were confined to a certain time, as my station in the women's ward, compelled a separation by ten o'clock, at which hour, the wards are separately locked.

At one of these meetings I was very near being turned out of the prison, as a strange; having accepted the office of president on a club-night, I equipped myself in a suit of men's clothes, and took the chair. After passing a few pleasant hours in the midst of our singing, smoking, and drinking, the time of separation arrived; when returning to the women's side, I was followed in by Mr. White, the principal turnkey, who asked my business, and mistaking me for a stranger, visiting some of the prisoners, conducted me into the lobby in order to turn me out.

But on my remonstrance that I was a prisoner, and telling my name, he threatened to send me to the felons' side, for attempting an escape in disguise; to which purpose he went and informed Mr. Kirby, the keeper, who shortly after coming into the lobby, I explained to him the whole of the transaction, adding, that having been used to a male dress in defence of my country, I thought I was sufficiently entitled to wear the same whenever I thought proper; at the same time shewing him the wounds I had received. He directed Mr. White to conduct me to the women's side as usual, and in a day or two, sent for me to relate to him the whole of my adventures, with which he seemed so well pleased, that he sent for me two or three times after when he had company, from whom I received some handsome presents.

I was advised to petition the Society for the relief of persons confined for small debts, and having obtained the form of a letter I should send, got it conveyed, with respectable vouchers as to the truth of my memorial. Five pounds was sent to Mr. Kirby for the purpose of settling the debt, but if the plaintiff refused that sum, it was to be returned to that charitable institution. Mrs. Nicklin, was, however, too good a judge to refuse so good an offer, and accordingly took the money, which was given to her friend Mr. Edmonds, on bringing my discharge. His expenses must have swallowed the greatest part of the above sum; and my landlady was well off in not being troubled herself by her own attorney, which must have been the case, if she had refused the sum offered, as I was determined to have sued her as soon as I could, for the sixpences.

My time in Newgate was rendered more comfortable than I had any reason to expect, from the constant attention of a female who had lived with me some time previous to my being arrested, for when no longer in my power to support her in the way I had been accustomed, instead of quitting me, she remained in the prison, and by needlework she obtained, contributed greatly to my support. She has continued with me ever since, and remains a constant friend in every change I have since experienced.

By an accidental mistake in arranging the notes I had made in the course of my narrative, the annexed circumstamces appear out of the order they should have been inserted; in order to rectify, as far as possible, the defect, I have referred back to the leading occurrences, with which they are connected.

★★★★★★

When I was about nine years of age, my sister took me from Chester to Trevalyn, on a visit for a few days; I had taken her to be my mother; and whenever speaking to her, called her as such. One day while in her own room she opened a kind of cabinet, and taking a miniature of a lady from a drawer. I asked her who it was. She burst into tears and told me she was not my mother, but that lady was, represented in the picture; whose daughter she also was, and my only surviving sister; and would endeavour to discharge the duty of both in herself towards me. The miniature represented a female of small size and very delicate appearance, with a remarkable blue spot on the forehead between the eyes; which though I never saw it afterwards, is so strongly imprinted on my mind, that nothing has been able to erase from my memory.

My sister was so much agitated on the occasion, as not to have told me my mother's name and family, of which I remain in ignorance to the present hour; though I have been informed of a family to whom my mother belonged, whose name, I do not think proper to make use of, not having as I think sufficient authority to assert as proof.

★★★★★★

While on board the *Vesuvius*, we encountered a most tremendous storm, in which I was employed on an occasion that I can never think of, without reflecting, how much hardship in youth, a human being can sustain. It was necessary for someone on board, to go to the jib-boom, to catch the jib-sheet, which in the gale had got loose. The continual lunging of the ship rendered this duty particularly hazardous, and not a seaman on board, but rejected this office. I acting on board in the capacity of midshipman, though I never received pay on board this ship, but as a common man. I mention this circumstance only, that it was not my particular duty to have undertaken the task, which on the refusal of several who were asked, and the preservation of us all depending on this exertion, I voluntarily undertook the charge.

On reaching the jib-boom, I was under the necessity of lashing myself fast to it; for the ship every minute making a fresh lunge, without such a precaution I should inevitably have been washed away, the surges continually breaking over me. I suffered an uninterrupted wash and fatigue for six hours, before I could quit the post I had so willingly occupied. But danger over, a sailor has little thought of reflections: and my messmates who had witnessed the perilous danger I was placed in, passed it off as a joke, "that I had only been *sipping sea-broth*;" but it was broth of a quality that though most seamen relish, yet few I imagine would like to take in the quantity I was compelled."

★★★★★★

The following anecdote, roused reflections which led me to seek a regular employment, and caused my application to Mr. Loyer, by whom I was afterwards engaged.

With the money I had received from Captain Field, of the *Ariel*, I frequented the theatres and houses about Convent Garden, where I became known to persons of every description as a good companion. Among others, I had formed an acquaintance with Haines, the well-known highwayman, who some time after was hung in chains, on Hounslow Heath, for shooting one of the Bow Street officers, who was about to apprehend him. This man I did not know followed so dangerous an occupation; but one evening, when my cash was nearly exhausted, I met him at a well-known house in Covent Garden, known by the name of the Finish. Being out of spirits, he questioned me as to the cause; I told him, I had lived so freely since I came on shore, that my cash was quite exhausted, and I was racking my imagination to get a fresh supply. He clapped his hand on my shoulder and exclaimed, "D——n it, my fine fellow, I'll put you up to the best way in the world to get the supply you stand in need of."—we left the house, and while walking, he proposed I should join him on an excursion to take a purse on the road; and observing that my sailor's habit was not calculated for the occasion, he furnished me with money to buy buckskin small clothes, &c. necessary for the purpose.

The road we were to take was not settled, but our meeting was fixed for the next night; I got the buckskin small clothes at Ford's, in the Strand, and a pair of boots from Newcomb, in Pall Mall. At the hour appointed, I met Haines at a livery stable behind the New Church, in the Strand, and found him in company with six more persons, all of whom I understood had met on the same business, though intending to take different roads. I was to accompany Haines, who furnished me with a pair of pistols, which he told me cost three guineas; when everything was ready for our departure, a sudden recollection of the danger and dishonour of this undertaking, providentially came to my aid; and I informed Haines how very reluctant I was to break an engagement, or my word in any particular, yet when I considered the consequence of the business in hand, I could not think of accompanying him, however far I had gone on the occasion; at the same time remarked, it was not the danger of the enterprise I dreaded, but the certain shame attached to a dishonourable action.

The principles of a state of warfare I should not mind, but never deliberately would act the part of a *Pirate*. He endeavoured to divert my resolution, and seemed very mad and inclined to quarrel, which I think was only stopped by a knowledge of the situation he stood in. I left the place congratulating myself on so narrow an escape, without farther opposition; though I saw Haines afterwards, he never took the least notice of the affair, and I took care for the future what company I got connected with."

★★★★★★

About the time of my working at Mr. Loyer's, I got acquainted in my male dress, with a person that informed me he was Vice-grand of a lodge of Odd Fellows, held at the Harlequin, near the stage-door of Drury Lane Theatre. This person discovering in me, a conviviality, suitable to such an undertaking, proposed my becoming one of their members; and as there was to be a meeting of the Lodge that evening, he said he would propose me as a new member. I readily accepting his offer, we adjourned to the place, where I went through the whole of the forms used on such occasions, and became a free member of the society of Odd Fellows, Lodge 21. Neither the person who introduced me, nor any of the members knowing my sex. It is the boast of free-masonry, that they never had more than one female belonging to their institution (namely, Queen Elizabeth); and I think I may fairly challenge any Lodge of Odd Fellows, to produce another female member: it being generally thought that there is not a female in England (myself excepted) belonging to this society.

I omitted to relate while on board the Crown transport, Captain Bishop; on our voyage to St. Domingo after the storm we suffered in, for want of provisions and water, we put in for repairs, up the windward passage, on the Musquito shore, and on one of the islands that distinguish this place, the boatswain and part of the ship's company, seven in number, of which I was one, went on shore to forage, and perceiving a bear, which the boatswain said was of the hyena kind, approaching us in a retrograde position, he fired at it when near us, and killed it. Having been so long kept on scanty allowance, we immediately opened our prize, and took out the heart, for fresh provision: the hams we conveyed on board, and committed them to the pickle tub for curing.

Before quitting the island, we proceeded farther on search after water, and fell in with a party of the barbarous natives, who make a practice of scalping the unfortunate victims that fall into their hands. These people approaching us in a menacing manner, we fired on them, and killed one, on which the remainder fled with precipitation towards the sea. On coming up to the dead man, we found that he was naked, except a wisp round his body, like a hay-band; his hair was long, black, and strong as horse hair, and in height, about six feet and proportionably lusty. He was armed with a tomahawk, or scalping hatchet, with which every one of his companions that fled were each furnished, and no more clad than their deceased friend. These weapons hung dangling to their hay-band, like girdles, which we observed from some of the party not having taken them in their hand for use; these people were of a tawny complexion.

At the time of my employ by Mr. Loyer, I put on my seaman's dress and accompanied the procession, when their Majesties went to St. Paul's, and the different colours of the enemy, were carried to be hung up in St. Paul's Church, as trophies of the victories obtained over their arms, by Howe, St. Vincent, and Duncan. I made part of Lord Howe's attendants with his colours, and, rode on the car, the chains of the bracelets Her Majesty wore on the occasion, were made by me, at Mr. Loyer's, by order from Messrs. Gray and Constable, Jewellers, of Sackville Street, Piccadilly.

It was my intention to insert the whole of the letters and family papers relative to my adventures, but have been deprived giving any at present, by an unforeseen accident, but shall be published in this work, as soon as ever recovered. The ensuing statement being the only cause of delay, will, I trust, be a sufficient excuse to every candid reader, by the difficulties I labour under; no other cause would have delayed their publication.

Soon after I quitted Newgate, my troubles again commenced. A Mr. E———, not far from Pump Court, in the Temple, employed me to wash, mend, &c. he becoming indebted to me thirty-eight pounds for that, and money, I had pledged my wearing apparel to lend him, though I have reason to think he is a man of property, I was under the necessity of arresting him to recover the same. I had received five pounds, and a letter from him at the same time, saying, "he would settle with me honourably;" not keeping his word was the cause of the arrest, and being at this time in the greatest distress through his proceedings, and the want of money and clothes, I took lodgings at the house of Mr. Joseph Bradley, No. 19, Little St. Mary-le-bone street, who is butler, and has been for many years to a gentleman in Glouces-ter Place, Hyde Park Corner.

Being in arrear for one week's rent, five shillings and sixpence, Mrs. Bradley, his wife, stopped not only my trunk, containing the whole of my letters and papers, but some needlework I had to do for another person, which had she suffered me to carry home, would have nearly paid her demand. I summoned her for the work to Marlborough-street, but the magistrate saying, they had a right to stop all they could lay their hands on, I was advised to arrest Mr. Bradley in an action of trover, as being deprived of the work, which they still hold, with my family letters and papers, which would have proved my debt against Mr. E———. This advice I followed, and Mr. Bradley was arrested. In the meantime, Mr. E——— took the opportunity of entering a *non pros* to my action; by not having it in my power to produce the papers necessary to prove the debt, which will compel me to enter a fresh process against him as soon as I can recover my papers, when his must appear.

I employed Mr. Worley, an attorney at No. 25, in Well' Street, Oxford Road, who directly sued out a writ against Bradley, which by some means was not served on him that term; before the next, he was arrested at my suit, and gave bail to Mr. Weekly the officer, for his appearance, which was entered at the commencement of the term, in order to go to trial. My attorney, Mr. Worley, on whom I called several times, informed me, that he would let me know, when I should be wanted to attend, and in the mean time said, if I would procure two pounds, he would establish me as a pauper, that I might proceed, without a necessity for more money. The above sum a gentleman advanced me for the purpose, and on my paying it into Mr. Worley's hands, he said, he would immediately proceed in the cause, and told me it would come on the present term.

The money I gave him on Wednesday, April 11th, 1804, and called by his appointment on Friday the 13th; not seeing him, I called the next day with no better success; as he told me it certainly would come on the present term. I became extremely anxious to see him, and called on Monday 16th, still I could not meet with him, and continued til twelve o'clock at night in the neighbourhood, calling at his house four times during that period. The only answer I could get, was, he had not been at home that day.

The next morning, April the 17th, I called and saw him, when he told me my action had suffered a *non-pros* on the 7th of March. Though I have repeatedly seen him before and since that time, he never informed me of the circumstance till that moment, by which I was deprived going to trial. Greatly shocked and disappointed, I told him I should inform the gentleman from whom I had received the money, the whole of the transaction; on which he waited on Mr. Worley, and was informed the money I had given him, he had carried to my account. Thus situated, with only part of my letters in my own possession, it is out of my power to give them at present, but having the promise of a friend to see me righted, Mr. Bradley, unless inclined to give my papers up, must be served with another process to compel him.

Nothing but troubles and misfortunes for the two last years of my life, having occurred, and followed me step by step, I have only to apologise to my readers, for any deviation from the paths of propriety, which only to my feelings, could have happened by the greatest necessity, and the deepest distress. I trust that I shall gain their pity, rather than censure, when I assert, had I been brought up in a workhouse, or any other situation to have gained my bread in the most humble manner, I should have preferred it, to the number of misfortunes and difficulties, I have been doomed to encounter, as my wounds and other afflictions have rendered me incapable of almost every exertion to procure a livelihood.

Having described as minutely as possible, the leading circumstances of my adventures, I submit the whole to the decision of my readers, with a solemn assurance, that in no particular have I advanced anything but matters of fact; which, if they should in any way serve as a lesson to future guardians and those under their care, in avoiding the troubles I have experienced, will answer one end to which they were made public by an unfortunate sufferer,

Mary Ann Talbot

MARY ANNE TALBOT
ALIAS
JOHN TAYLOR

The Life of Mary Read

Now we are to begin a history full of surprising turns and adventures, I mean, that of Mary Read and Anne Bonny, *alias* Bonn, which were the true names of these two pirates, the odd incidents of their rambling lives are such, that some may be tempted to think the whole story no better than a novel or romance, but since it is supported by many thousand witnesses, I mean the people of Jamaica, who were present at their trials, and heard the story of their lives, upon the first discovery of their sex, the truth of it can be no more contested, than that there were such men in the world, as Roberts and Black-beard, who were pirates.

Mary Read was born in England, her mother was married young, to a man who used the sea, who going a voyage soon after their marriage, left her with child, which child proved to be a boy. As to the husband, whether he was cast away, or died in the voyage, Mary Read could not tell; but however, he never returned more. Nevertheless, the mother, who was young and airy, met with an accident, which has often happened to women who are young, and do not take a great deal of care; which was, she soon proved with child again, without a husband to father it, but how, or by whom, none but herself could tell, for she carried a pretty good reputation among her neighbours. Finding her burthen grow, in order to conceal her shame, she takes a formal leave of her husband's relations, giving out, that she went to live with some friends of her own, in the country. Accordingly she went away, and carried with her her young son, at this time, not a year old. Soon after her departure her son died, but Providence in return, was pleased to give her a girl in his room, of which she was safely delivered, in her retreat, and this was our Mary Read.

Here the mother lived three or four years, till what money she had was almost gone; then she thought of returning to London, and considering that her husband's mother was in some circumstances, she did not doubt but to prevail upon her, to provide for the child, if she could but pass it upon her for the same. But the changing a girl into a boy, seemed a difficult piece of work, and how to deceive an experienced old woman, in such a point, was altogether as impossible. However, she ventured to dress it up as a boy, brought it to town, and presented it to her mother in law, as her husband's son. The old woman would have taken it, to have bred it up, but the mother pretended it would break her heart, to part with it so it was agreed betwixt them, that the child should live with the mother, and the supposed grandmother should allow a crown a week for its maintenance.

Thus the mother gained her point, she bred up her daughter as a boy, and when she grew up to some sense, she thought proper to let her into the secret of her birth, to induce her to conceal her sex. It happened that the grandmother died, by which means the subsistence that came from that quarter, ceased, and they were more and more reduced in their circumstances, wherefore she was obliged to put her daughter out, to wait on a French lady, as a foot-boy, being now thirteen years of age. Here she did not live long, for growing bold and strong, and having also a roving mind, she entered herself on board a man of war, where she served some time, then quitted it, went over into Flanders, and carried arms in a regiment of foot, as a cadet. And though upon all actions, she behaved herself with a great deal of bravery, yet she could not get a commission, they being generally bought and sold; therefore she quitted the service, and took on in a regiment of horse.

She behaved so well in several engagements, that she got the esteem of all her officers, but her comrade who was a Flemings happening to be a handsome young fellow, she falls in love with him, and from that time, grew a little more negligent in her duty, so that, it seems, Mars and Venus could not be served at the same time. Her arms and accoutrements which were always kept in the best order, were quite neglected: 'tis true, when her comrade was ordered out upon a party, she used to go without being commanded, and frequently run herself into danger, where she had no business, only to be near him. The rest of the troopers little suspecting the secret cause which moved her to this behaviour, fancied her to be mad, and her comrade himself could not account for this strange alteration in her. But love is ingenious, and as they lay in the same tent, and were constantly together, she found a way of letting him discover her sex, without appearing that it was done with design.

He was much surprised at what he found out, and not a little pleased, taking it for granted, that he should have a mistress solely to himself, which is an unusual thing in a camp, since there is scarce one of those campaign ladies, that is ever true to a troop or company; so that he thought of nothing but gratifying his passions with very little ceremony. But he found himself strangely mistaken, for she proved very reserved and modest, and resisted all his temptations, and at the same time was so obliging and insinuating in her carriage, that she quite changed his purpose, so far from thinking of making her his mistress, now courted her for a wife.

This was the utmost wish of her heart, in short, they exchanged promises, and when the campaign was over, and the regiment marched into winter quarters, they bought woman's apparel for her, with such money as they could make up betwixt them, and were publicly married.

The story of two troopers marrying each other, made a great noise, so that several officers were drawn by curiosity to assist at the ceremony, and they agreed among themselves that every one of them should make a small present to the bride, towards house-keeping, in consideration of her having been their fellow soldier. Thus being set up, they seemed to have a desire of quitting the service, and settling in the world. The adventure of their love and marriage had gained them so much favour, that they easily obtained their discharge, and they immediately set up an eating house or ordinary, which was the Sign of the Three Horse-Shoes, near the Castle of Breda, where they soon run into a good trade, a great many officers eating with them constantly.

But this happiness lasted not long, for the husband soon died, and the Peace of Ryswick being concluded, there was no resort of officers to Breda, as usual; so that the widow having little or no trade, was forced to give up housekeeping, and her substance being by degrees quite spent, she again assumes her man's apparel, and going into Holland, there takes on in a regiment of foot, quartered in one of the frontier towns. Here she did not remain long, there was no likelihood of preferment in time of peace, therefore she took a resolution of seeking her fortune another way, and withdrawing from the regiment, ships herself on board of a vessel bound for the West-Indies.

It happened this ship was taken by English pirates, and Mary Read was the only English person on board, they kept her amongst them, and having plundered the ship, let it go again. After following this trade for some time, the King's Proclamation came out, and was published in all parts of the West-Indies, for pardoning such pirates, who should voluntarily surrender themselves by a certain day therein mentioned. The crew of Mary Read took the benefit of this proclamation, and having surrendered, lived quietly on shore. But money beginning to grow short, and hearing that Captain Woods Rogers, governor of the Island of Providence, was fitting out some privateers to cruise against the Spaniards, she with several others embarked for that island, in order to go upon the privateering account, being resolved to make her fortune one way or other.

These privateers were no sooner sailed out, but the crews of some of them, who had been pardoned, rose against their commanders, and turned themselves to their old trade. In this number was Mary Read. It is true, she often declared, that the life of a pirate was what she always abhorred, and went into it only upon compulsion, both this time, and before, intending to quit it, whenever a fair opportunity should offer itself. Yet some of the evidence against her, upon her trial, who were forced men, and had failed with her, deposed upon oath, that in times of action, no person amongst them were more resolute, or ready to board or undertake anything that was hazardous, as she and Anne Bonny. Particularly at the time they were attacked and taken, when they came to close quarters, none kept the deck except Mary Read and Anne Bonny, and one more; upon which, she, Mary Read, called to those under deck, to come up and fight like men. And finding they did not stir, fired her arms down the hold amongst them, killing one, and wounding others.

This was part of the evidence against her, which she denied which, whether true or no, thus much is certain, that she did not want bravery, nor indeed was she less remarkable for her modesty, according to her notions of virtue. Her sex was not so much as suspected by any person on board, till Anne Bonny, who was not altogether so reserved in point of chastity, took a particular liking to her. In short, Anne Bonny took her for a handsome young fellow, and for some reasons best known to herself, first discovered her sex to Mary Read. Mary Read knowing what she would be at, and being very sensible of her own incapacity that way, was forced to come to a right understanding with her, and so to the great disappointment of Anne Bonny, she let her know she was a woman also. But this intimacy so disturbed Captain Rackam, who was the lover and gallant of Anne Bonny, that he grew furiously jealous, so that he told Anne Bonny, he would cut her new lover's throat, therefore, to quiet him, she let him into the secret also.

Captain Rackam, (as he was enjoined,) kept, the thing a secret from all the ship's company, yet, notwithstanding all her cunning and reserve, love found her out in this disguise, and hindered her from forgetting her sex. In their cruise they took a great number of ships belonging to Jamaica, and other parts of the West-Indies, bound to and from England, and when ever they meet any good artist, or other person that might be of any great use to their company, if he was not willing to enter, it was their custom to keep him by force. Among these was a young fellow of a most engaging behaviour, or, at least, he was so in the eyes of Mary Read, who became so smitten with his person and address, that she could neither rest, night or day. But as there is nothing more ingenious than love, it was no hard matter for her, who had before been practiced in these wiles, to find a way to let him discover her sex. She first insinuated herself into his liking, by talking against the life of a pirate, which he was altogether averse to, so they became mess-mates and strict companions. When she found he had a friendship for her, as a man, she suffered the discovery to be made, by carelessly shewing her breasts, which were very white.

The young fellow, who was made of flesh and blood, had his curiosity and desire so raised by this sight, that he never ceased importuning her, till she confessed what she was. Now begins the scene of love; as he had a liking and esteem for her, under her supposed character, it was now turned into fondness and desire. Her passion was no less violent than his, and perhaps she expressed it, by one of the most generous actions that ever love inspired. It happened this young fellow had a quarrel with one of the pirates, and their ship then lying at an anchor, near one of the islands, they had appointed to go ashore and fight, according to the custom of the pirates. Mary Read, was to the last degree uneasy and anxious, for the fate of her lover; she would not have had him refuse the challenge, because, she could not bear the thoughts of his being branded with cowardice on the other side, she dreaded the event, and apprehended the fellow might be too hard for him.

When love once enters into the breast of one who has any sparks of generosity, it; stirs the heart up to the most noble actions. In this dilemma, she shewed, that she feared more for his life than she did for her own for she took a resolution of quarrelling with this fellow herself, and having challenged him ashore, she appointed the time two hours sooner than that, when he was to meet her lover, where she fought him at sword and pistol, and killed him upon the spot.

It is true, she had fought before, when she had been insulted by some of those fellows, but now it was altogether in her lover's cause, she stood as it were betwixt him and death, as if she could not live without him. If he had no regard for her before, this action would have bound him to her forever, but there was no occasion for ties or obligations, his inclination towards her was sufficient. In fine, they applied their troth to each other, which Mary Read said, she looked upon to be as good a marriage, in conscience, as if it had been done by a minister in church, and to this was owing her great belly, which she pleaded to save her life.

She declared she had never committed adultery or fornication with any man, she commended the justice of the court, before which she was tried, for distinguishing the nature of their crimes. Her husband, as she called him, with several others, being acquitted, and being asked, who he was, she would not tell, but, said he was an honest man, and had no inclination to such practices, and that they had both resolved to leave the pirates the first opportunity, and apply themselves to some honest livelihood.

It is no doubt, but many had compassion for her, yet the court could not avoid finding her guilty; for among other things, one of the evidences against her, deposed, that being taken by Rackam, and detained some time on board, he fell accidentally into discourse with Mary Read. Taking her for a young man, he asked her what pleasure she could have in being concerned in such enterprise, where her life was continually in danger, by fire or sword, and not only so, but she must be sure of dying an ignominious death, if she should be taken alive.—She answered, that as to hanging, she thought it no great hardship, for, were it not for that, every cowardly fellow would turn pirate, and so infest the seas, that men of courage must starve:—That if it was put to the choice of the pirates, they would not have the punishment less than death, the fear of which, kept some dastardly rogues honest that many of those who are now cheating the widows and orphans, and oppressing their poor neighbours, who have no money to obtain justice, would then rob at sea, and the ocean would be crowded with rogues, like the land, and no merchant would venture out; so that the trade, in a little time, would not be worth following.

Being found quick with child, as has been observed, her execution was respited, and it is possible she would have found favour, but she was seized with a violent fever, soon after her trial, of which she died in prison.

The Life of Anne Bonny

As we have been more particular in the lives of these two women, than those of other pirates, it is incumbent on us, as a faithful historian, to begin with their birth. Anne Bonny was born at a town near Cork, in the kingdom of Ireland, her father an attorney at law, but Anne was not one of his legitimate issue, which seems to cross an old proverb, which says, that *bastards have the best luck* her father was a married man, and his wife having been brought to bed, contracted an illness in her lying in, and in order to recover her health, she was advised to remove for change of air. The place she chose, was a few miles distance from her dwelling, where her husband's mother lived.

Here she sojourned some time, her husband staying at home, to follow his affairs. The servant-maid, whom she left to look after the house, and attend the family, being a handsome young woman, was courted by a young man of the same town, who was a tanner. This tanner used to take his opportunities, when the family was out of the way, of coming to pursue his courtship, and being with the maid one day as she was employed in the household business, not having the fear of God before his eyes, he takes his opportunity, when her back was turned, of whipping three silver spoons into his pocket. The maid soon missed the spoons, and knowing that nobody had been in the room, but herself and the young man, since she saw them last, she charged him with taking them. He very stiffly denied it, upon which she grew outrageous, and threatened to go to a constable, in order to carry him before a justice of peace. These menaces frightened him out of his wits, well knowing he could not stand search wherefore he endeavoured to pacify her, by desiring her to examine the drawers and other places, and perhaps she might find them.

In this time he slips into another room, where the maid usually lay, and puts the spoons betwixt the sheets, and then makes his escape by a back door, concluding she must find them, when she went to bed, and so next day he might pretend he did it only to frighten her, and the thing might be laughed off for a jest.

As soon as she missed him, she gave over her search, concluding he had carried them off, and went directly to the constable, in order to have him apprehended. The young man was informed, that a constable had been in search of him, but he regarded it but little, not doubting but all would be well next day. Three or four days passed, and still he was told, the constable was upon the hunt for him, this made him lie concealed. He could not comprehend the meaning of it, he imagined no less, than that the maid had a mind to convert the spoons to her own use, and put the robbery upon him.

It happened, at this time, that the mistress being perfectly recovered of her late indisposition, was returned home, in company with her mother-in-law. The first news she heard, was of the loss of the spoons, with the manner how, the maid telling her, at the same time, that the young man was run away. The young fellow had intelligence of the mistress's arrival, and considering with himself, that he could never appear again in his business, unless this matter was got over, and she being a good natured woman, he took a resolution of going directly to her, and of telling her the whole story, only with this difference, that he did it for a jest.

The mistress could scarce believe it, however, she went directly to the maid's room, and turning down the bedclothes, there, to her great surprise, found the three spoons upon this she desired the young man to go home and mind his business, for he should have no trouble about it.

The mistress could not imagine the meaning of this, she never had found the maid guilty of any pilfering, and therefore it could not enter her head, that she designed to steal the spoons herself; upon the whole, she concluded the maid had not been in her bed, from the time the spoons were missed, she grew immediately jealous upon it, and suspected, that the maid supplied her place with her husband, during her absence, and this was the reason why the spoons were no sooner found.

She called to mind several actions of kindness, her husband had shewed the maid. Things that passed unheeded by, when they happened, but now she had got that tormentor, jealousy, in her head, amounted to proofs of their intimacy. Another circumstance which strengthened the whole, was, that though her husband knew she was to come home that day, and had had no communication with her in four months, which was before her last lying in, yet he took an opportunity of going out of town that morning, upon some flight pretence:—All these things put together, confirmed her in her jealousy.

As women seldom forgive injuries of this kind, she thought of discharging her revenge upon the maid. In order to this, she leaves the spoons where she found them, and orders the maid to put clean sheets upon the bed, telling her, she intended to lie there herself that night, because her mother-in-law was to lie in her bed, and that she (the maid) must lie in another part of the house. The maid in making the bed, was surprised with the sight of the spoons, but there were very good reasons, why it was not proper for her to tell where she found them, therefore she takes them up, puts them in her trunk, intending to leave them in some place, where they might be found by chance.

The mistress, that everything might look to be done without design, lies that night in the maid's bed, little dreaming of what an adventure it would produce. After she had been a bed some time, thinking on what had passed, for jealousy kept her awake, she heard somebody enter the room. At first she apprehended it to be thieves, and was so frightened, she had not courage enough to call out, but when she heard these words, 'Mary, are you awake?' she knew it to be her husband's voice. Then her fright was over, yet she made no answer, least he should find her out, if she spoke, therefore she resolved to counterfeit sleep, and take what followed.

The husband came to bed, and that night played the vigorous lover, but one thing stopped the diversion on the wife's side, which was, the reflection that it was not designed for her. However she was very passive, and bore it like a Christian. Early before day, she stole out of bed, leaving him asleep, and went to her mother-in-law, telling her what had passed, not forgetting how he had used her, as taking her for the maid. The husband also stole out, not thinking it convenient to be caught in that room. In the meantime, the revenge of the mistress was strongly against the maid, and without considering, that to her she owed the diversion of the night before, and that *one good turn should deserve another one* sent for a constable, and charged her with stealing the spoons. The maid's trunk was broke open, and the spoons found, upon which she was carried before a justice of peace, and by him committed to goal.

The husband loitered about till twelve a clock at noon, then comes home, pretended he was just come to town. As soon as he heard what had passed, in relation to the maid, he fell into a great passion with his wife this set the thing into a greater flame. The mother takes the wife's part against her own son, insomuch that the quarrel increasing, the mother and wife took horse immediately, and went back to the mother's house, and the husband and wife never bedded together after.

The maid lay a long time in the prison, it being near half a year to the assizes, but before it happened, it was discovered she was with child. When she was arraigned at the bar, she was discharged for want of evidence. The wife's conscience touched her, and as she did not believe the maid guilty of any theft, except that of love, she did not appear against her. Soon after her acquittal, she was delivered of a girl.

But what alarmed the husband most, was, that it was discovered the wife was with child also, he taking it for granted, he had had no intimacy with her, since her last lying in, grew jealous of her, in his turn, and made this a handle to justify himself, for his usage of her, pretending now he had suspected her long, but that here was proof. She was delivered of twins, a boy and a girl.

The mother fell ill, sent to her son to reconcile him to his wife, but he would not hearken to it therefore she made a will, leaving all she had in the hands of certain trustees, for the use of the wife and two children lately born, and died a few days after.

This was an ugly turn upon him, his greatest dependence being upon his mother; however, his wife was kinder to him than he deserved, for she made him a yearly allowance out of what was left, though they continued to live separate. It lasted near five years ; at this time having a great affection for the girl he had by his maid, he had a mind to take it home, to live with him; but as all the town knew it to be a girl, the better to disguise the matter from them, as well as from his wife. He had it put into breeches, as a boy, pretending it was a relation's child he was to breed up to be his clerk.

The wife heard he had a little boy at home he was very fond of, but as she did not know any relation of his that had such a child, she employed a friend to enquire further into it. This person by talking with the child, found it to be a girl, discovered that the servant-maid was its mother, and that the husband still kept up his correspondence with her.

Upon this intelligence, the wife being unwilling that her children's money should go towards the maintenance of bastards, stopped the allowance. The husband enraged, in a kind of revenge, takes the maid home, and lives with her publicly, to the great scandal of his neighbours. But he soon found the bad effect of it, for by degrees lost

58

his practice, so that he saw plainly he could not live there, therefore he thought of removing, and turning what effects he had into ready money; he goes to Cork, and there with his maid and daughter embarks for Carolina.

At first he followed the practice of the law in that province, but afterwards fell into merchandise, which proved more successful to him, for he gained by it sufficient to purchase a considerable plantation. His maid, who passed for his wife, happened to die, after which his daughter, our Anne Bonny, now grown up, kept his house. She was of a fierce and courageous temper, wherefore, when she lay under condemnation, several stories were reported of her, much to her disadvantage, as that she had killed an English servant-maid once in her passion with a case-knife, while she looked after her father's house, but upon further enquiry, I found this story to be groundless. It was certain she was so robust, that once, when a young fellow would have lain with her against her will, she beat him so that he lay ill of it a considerable time.

While she lived with her father, she was looked upon as one that would be a good fortune, wherefore it was thought her father expected a good match for her. But she spoilt all, for without his content, she marries a young fellow, who belonged to the sea, and was not worth a groat which provoked her father to such a degree, that he turned her out of doors. Upon which the young fellow, who married her, finding himself disappointed in his expectation, shipped himself and wife, for the island of Providence, expecting employment there.

Here she became acquainted with Rackam the pirate, who making courtship to her, soon found means of withdrawing her affections from her husband, so that she consented to elope from him, and go to sea with Rackam in men's clothes. She was as good as her word, and after she had been at sea some time, she proved with child, and beginning to grow big, Rackam landed her on the island of Cuba, and recommending her there to some friends of his, they took care of her, till she was brought to bed. When she was up and well again, he sent for her to bear him company.

The King's Proclamation being out, for pardoning of pirates, he took the benefit of it, and surrendered afterwards being sent upon the privateering account, he returned to his old trade, as has been already hinted in the story of Mary Read. In all these expeditions, Anne Bonny bore him company, and when any business was to be done in their way, nobody was more forward or courageous than she, and particularly when they were taken. She and Mary Read, with one more, were all the persons that durst keep the deck, as has been before hinted.

Her father was known to a great many gentlemen, planters of Jamaica, who had dealt with him, and among whom he had a good reputation and some of them, who had been in Carolina, remembered to have seen her in his house, wherefore they were inclined to shew her favour. But the action of leaving her husband was an ugly circumstance against her. The day that Rackam was executed, by special favour, he was admitted to see her but all the comfort she gave him, was, *that she was sorry to see him there, but if he had fought like a man, he need not have been hanged like a dog.*

She was continued in prison, to the time of her lying in, and afterwards reprieved from time to time but what is become of her since, we cannot tell, only this we know, that she was not executed.

Ann Jane Thornton: The Female Sailor

American Broadside

In the month of February 1835 this interesting girl arrived at Fresh Wharf London bridge, on board the *Sarah*; her sex having been discovered a few days previous. Of course so singular circumstance as that of a young female sailor could not long be kept a secret; and, as always the case, the most exaggerated reports were immediately propagated.

At length this extraordinary history reached the ears of the Lord Mayor, who with the greatest humanity, ordered one of the police to ascertain the particulars of the case and see whether she was ill used. The officer brought her to the Lord Mayor to whom she related the following interesting particulars:—

She said her name was Ann Jane Thornton, that she was in the 17th year of her age. Her father being a widower took her and the rest of the family from Gloucestershire, where she was born to Donegal, when six years old, where her father now resides. She regretted leaving home, as it must have caused him many a sorrowful hour, he being always affectionate to her.

When she was only 13 years old she met Captain Alexander Burk, an Englishman but whose father resided in New York, and before she was 15 they became strongly attached to each other. Soon afterwards Alexander Burk was obliged to go to New York, and she resolved to follow him. She quitted her father's house, accompanied by a maid-servant and a boy, and having acquired a cabin boy's dress, she obtained a passage direct to America. By degrees she became reconciled to her new situation, and when she arrived in New York she hastened to the father of her sweetheart, where she learnt he was dead. Disconsolate as she was, she hastened from East Point in North America, to St. Andrew's a distance of 70 miles through the woods alone, walking all the way on foot.

She then obtained the situation of cook and steward on board the *Adelaide*, and next in the *Rover*, in which latter vessel she sailed to St. Andrew's where she fell in with the *Sarah*, whose captain, M'Intyre, engaged her, under the name of Jim Thornton, as cook and steward, and in which ship she arrived in the port of London. One day as she was washing in her berth, with her jacket loose in the front, one of the crew caught an accidental view of her bosom, and threatened to tell the captain unless she had sexual intercourse with him. She refused, and he revealed her sex to the captain, he turned her out to work amongst the men, by whom she upon all occasions was most grossly insulted.

Captain M'Intyre later told the *Times:*—

I could scarcely credit the mate when he told me of it. I can bear testimony to the extraordinary propriety of her conduct and I ask again whether I have not acted properly towards her.

She did the duty of a seaman without a murmur and had infi-nitely a better use of her hands than her tongue. She performed to admiration. She would run up the top gallant-sail in any sort of weather and we had a severe passage. Poor girl, she had a hard time of it, she suffered greatly from the wet but she bore it all excellently and was a capital seaman.

For 31 months she had been engaged in these remarkable adven-tures and participated in the most severe toils of the crews of which she performed a part, with the greatest propriety and decorum.

She returned to Donegal in April 1835, after the Lord Mayor had made inquiries and discovered she still had a sister living there, but her father had himself emigrated to America. A newspaper in Ballyshanon reported:—

A vast crowd collected to see her, but the sailor hurried to the house of her sister, in the back lane. We were fortunate enough to have seen the young woman. She is now quite tired of the sea she says she would not join a ship again for £500 a year as it is the most wretched life imaginable. She says she will never marry.

She was granted a pension of £10 a year by King William IV and a farm rent free by a Mr. Andrew Murray. She married a friend in February 1836 who rescued her from a forced marriage. She died in 1877.

The following song is based on her story:—

Good people give attention and listen to my song;
I will unfold a circumstance that does to love belong;
Concerning of a pretty maid who ventur'd we are told
Across the briny ocean as a female sailor bold.

Her name was Ann Jane Thornton, as you presently shall hear,
And also that she was born in fam'd Gloucestershire;
Her father now lives in Ireland, respected we are told,
And grieving for his daughter—this female sailor bold.

She was courted by a captain when not fifteen years of age,
And to be joined in holy wedlock this couple did engage,
But the captain was bound to America, as I will now unfold,
And she followed him o'er the ocean did this female sailor bold.

She dress'd herself in sailors clothes and was overcome with joy
When with a captain she did engage to serve as cabin boy,
And when New York in America this fair maid did behold
She determined to seek her true love did this female sailor bold.

Then to her true loves fathers she hastened with speed,
When the news that she did hear most dreadful indeed,
That her love had been dead some time they to her did unfold
Which very near broke the heart of this female sailor bold.

Some thousand miles she was from home from friends far away
Alone she travelled seventy miles thro' woods in North America
Bereft of all her kindred nor no parent to behold,
In anguish she cried my true love did this female sailor bold.

Then she went on board the *Adelaide*, to cross the troubled wave
And in storms of hail and gales of wind she did all dangers brave
She served as cook and steward in the *Adelaide* we are told
Then sailed on board the *Rover* did the female sailor bold.

From St Andrew's in America this fair maid did set sail,
In a vessel called the *Sarah* and brav'd many a stormy gale
She did her duty like a man did reef and steer we're told
By the captain she was respected well—the female sailor bold.

With pitch and tar her hands were hard, tho' once like velvet soft
She weighed the anchor, heav'd the lead and boldly went aloft

Just one and thirty months she braved the tempest we are told
And always did her duty did the female sailor bold.

'Twas in the month of February eighteen hundred thirty five,
She in the port of London in the *Sarah* did arrive;
Her sex was then discovered which the secret did unfold,
And the captain gaz'd in wonder on the female sailor bold.

At the Mansion-House she appear'd before the Lord Mayor,
And in the public papers then the reasons did appear,
Why she did leave her father and her native land she told,
To brave the stormy ocean, did this female sailor bold.

It was to seek her lover that sailed across the main,
Thro' love she did encownter storms tempest wind and rain.
It was love caused all her troubles and hardships we are told;
May she rest at home contented now the female sailor bold.

The Female Shipwright
By Mary Lacy

PREFACE

The reality of the facts contained in the following history will, it is presumed, conduce in a great measure to recommend the perusal of it to the public; and it will, I doubt not, with every candid and considerate reader, prove a sufficient apology for the inaccuracies of stile and sentiment which I may be justly chargeable with as the author, that I laboured under many inconveniences in collecting the various materials which compose it. The great number of incidents related therein are presented to public inspection in a plain and simple garb, that being judged the most suitable dress for a narrative of this kind.

The reader will find herein:—

1. A circumstantial account of what happened to me during my childhood, wherein will appear many evident tokens of that restless and untractable disposition in an early period of life, which gave rise to all my succeeding adventures and misfortunes.

2. The method made use for leaving my parents, by disguising myself in man's apparel, principally for the sake of withdrawing myself from the company of a young man, for whom I found I had conceived too great an attachment, and who was the primary, though involuntary cause of my departure. The uncommon embarrassments and difficulties I struggled with during the first four years of my service, in order to conceal my sex when at sea, where I was almost continually in company with 700 men for that time, without incurring the least suspicion of being a woman: for which, and the many narrow escapes I afterwards had, I cannot but acknowledge myself indebted to the goodness of Divine Providence, who endued me with prudence and discretion to conduct myself under every circumstance, and carried me through all.

3. Of my serving seven years as an apprentice to a shipwright, with the numerous sufferings I endured from ill-treatment under different masters, and the various scenes of immorality and profaneness my situation amongst sea-faring people made me a constant, though disgusted, witness to.

4. The hardships I went through in being forced to cross the water at Gosport in the most inclement of seasons for the space of five years and a half; the severe labour I was employed in since that time, attended with illness, amidst the dreadful apprehensions of a discovery of my sex through the baseness of the woman who betrayed me.

It will not be amiss to conclude this address by explaining my motives for endeavouring to be as frequently as possible in the company of women, in the way of courtship; which were, In the first place, to avoid the conversation of the men, which I need not observe, was amongst those of this class especially, in many respects very offensive to a delicate ear: and, secondly, For the sake of affording me a more agreeable repast amongst persons of my own sex, many of whom, I am sorry to say, were too much addicted to evil practices by their unlawful commerce with the other, as will on many occasions appear in the course of the story.

Deptford, July 1, 1773.
M. Slade.

THE HISTORY OF THE FEMALE SHIPWRIGHT

After mentioning my maiden name, which was Mary Lacy, it will be proper to inform the reader, that I was born at Wickham, in the county of Kent, on the 12th of January, 1740; but had not been long in the world before my father and mother agreed to live at Ash, so that I knew little more of Wickham than I had learned from my parents, on which account Ash might almost be reckoned my native place.

My father and mother were poor, and forced to work very hard for their bread. They had one son and two daughters, of whom I was the eldest. At a proper time, my mother put me to school, to give me what learning she could, which kept me out of their way whilst they were at work; for being young, I was always in mischief; and my mother not having spare time sufficient to look after me, I had so much my own will, that when I came to have some knowledge, it was a difficult matter for them to keep me within proper bounds.

After I had learned my letters, I was admitted into a charity school, which was kept by one Mrs. R———n; and she, knowing my parents, took great pains to instruct me in reading. As I took my learning very fast, my mistress was the more careful of me; for she was indeed as a mother to me; and in these respects was more serviceable than my parents could possibly be. When I was old enough to learn to work, my mistress taught me to knit; which she perceiving me very fond of learning, employed me in knitting gloves, stockings, nightcaps, and such sort of work, so that I soon perfected myself in it; which I was more encouraged to, as my mistress rewarded me for every piece of knitting, and all the money I earned she reserved in a little box; so that when I wanted any thing, she would buy it for me. Thus, by the help of God and good friends, I was no great charge to my parents; for being always at school, my mistress set me about all manner of work in the house; so that, though young, I was very handy, and in a way of improvement.

About this time I used to go on errands for my neighbours, and help them what I could; but that practice, by occasioning me to go pretty much abroad in the streets, became very prejudicial to me; for I was thereby addicted to all manner of mischief, as will appear by the following instance: There was one C—h—e Cipp—r, about my age, that lived in Ash, with whom, when I could get out, I always kept company, and, when together, did many unjustifiable actions; for one day we took it into our heads to purloin a bridle and saddle out of the stable of one Mr. John R———n, butcher at Ash, who kept a little horse in a field about half a mile from the town.

This horse we caught, put the saddle and bridle on, and rode about the field till we were tired, and afterwards restored them to the place from whence we took them. I liked riding so well, that I never was easy but when among the horses; for I used to go to Mr. R—h—d—n, and say, "Master, shall I fetch your sheep up out of the field?" And if he wanted them, I immediately took the little horse, without saddle or bridle, and mounting on his back, set off as fast as the horse could go, thus running all hazards of my life; and was so wild and heedless, that if anybody took notice of my riding so fast, and told me I should fall off, and break my neck, my answer was, "Neck or nothing!" If I happened to fall, I did not care, for I was no sooner off than on again.

I then thought my mother was my greatest enemy; for she being a very passionate woman, used to beat me in such a manner, that the neighbours thought she would kill me. But after my crying was over, I was out of the doors again at my old tricks with my playfellows, and frequently staid out all day long, and never went home at all; for which I was afterwards sure to be corrected.

There was one Mrs. Bax that lived the next door to my mother, who every now and then wanted me to bring her something, and often caused me to be beat, so that I did not like her at all. But one morning she asked my mother, to let me fetch her a halfpenny loaf for her breakfast, which my mother ordered me to do. I went to bring the loaf; but thought within myself I would be even with her; and knowing she could not eat the crust, as I came home with it I eat out all the crumb, and putting the two crusts together again, carried it into her house, and laid it down, and then set off for the whole day; for I knew that if I went home I should be beat. When she had found out that I had eat the crumb of the loaf, she told my mother what I had done; but not finding me, my mother told her, that when I came home at night she would chastise me for it, which she accordingly did, and made me go to bed without any supper.

After this, my mother was determined to make me go to service, as soon as she could get a place for me, as she thought I grew worse by running about the streets; and my mistress where I went to school having seven children, the first place I had was with one of her daughters, whose name was Mary Richardson. I staid with her about a year and half, and then returned home to my mother; soon after which I went to school to learn to write.

After I had been at home about a year, I went to live with an elder sister of my former mistress. She was married to one Mr. Goodson, a shoemaker, who was set up in his business, and employed men to work for him. They both lived very happy together; and she had three children by him. But as it pleased God to take my master out of the world, his widow settled herself in a milliner's shop, she being capable of making everything she sold: by this prudent conduct my mistress did very well, and used me kindly, but I was at that time too insensible of the good treatment I met with. She learned me to work with my needle, which if I had but applied myself with proper care and industry, I should, in all probability, have escaped many of the unknown sorrows I afterwards suffered.

But, as is commonly the case, when young and inexperienced in the world, we are not aware of the calamities that may befall us as we advance in life. I was so very thoughtless and discontented, that I was always ill, or has some complaint or other to make; but what, I did not know; and would often go and tell my mother my grievances;

and, she having a tender heart, believed all I said, and took my part, which contributed to make me idle; and if my mistress said anything I did not like, though it was for my good, I used to go and represent it in an unfavourable light to my mother; for which behaviour if she had reprimanded or even beat me, I should have left off so childish a practice; and should rather have minded what my mistress said to me, and obeyed her. But being of a roving disposition, I never liked to be within doors; and if I could get out with the young child, I though myself happy; for if I staid within doors, I was idle, and studying what mischief I should do; so that my thoughts were never inclined to any good for myself.

My mistress married a second time to one Mr. Daniel Deverson, a shoemaker, and they lived very happy together; which I might have experienced the good effects of, had I not been of such an untowardly turn of mind; for I had now acquired such a fondness for dancing, that I used to get out of the house in the evening, and be dancing all the night long, which was the beginning of all my sorrow; for by this means I contracted an acquaintance with a new sweetheart, so that I never was contented but when in his company. But happening to be out one night at this pastime, the child cried that used to lie with me, and waked my mistress. She hearing the child cry, called to me, but receiving no answer, got up, and came into my room; but not finding me there, she thought I was gone to a house where a young man used to play on the violin; for she knew the young men and maids met at this house. When my mistress came to the house where I was, she found me very merry and happy; but when I saw her, I was very much surprised, and seemed very sorry for what I had done, because (as it was the first time I was discovered) she thought I had never served her so before; but I had been out time after time, though this was the first occasion of its being known.

The next morning, my mistress told me that I should do myself no good, by going on in this course of life, and gave me some very sea-sonable advice, if I had been but wise enough to think so; but I took it quite the contrary way, and thought I was not well used; whereupon we agreed to part. I was now about sixteen years of age; and have often since reflected that my mistress bore my misbehaviour and cross tem-per purely with a view to my advantage, and kept me so long with her for no other purpose, if I could but have thought so; for it is certain she wished me as well as if I had been one of her own children.

After leaving my mistress, I went home, as usual, to my father and mother. I now embraced all opportunities of going out to dance with my sweetheart; for when I was with him I imagined myself happy. But this young man did not perceive that I loved him so much; and it happened very unfortunately I did not tell any of my friends of it; which if I had done, it would probably have been better for me; for my mother would no doubt have persuaded me for my good. But I afterwards felt the bad effects of concealing this warm affection. I could not blame the young man, since he had never given me any reason so to do. Hereupon I was very unsettled in my mind, and unable to fix myself in any place; nevertheless, I carried it off as well as I could.

I had not been long at home, before one Mr. Daniel Stoaders at Ash wanted me to come and live with him; accordingly I went, and liked the place very well; and, had I been but contented, I might have lived there very comfortably. But my mind became continually disturbed and uneasy about this young man, who was the involuntary cause of all my trouble, which was aggravated by my happening to see him one day talk to a young woman: the thoughts of this made me so very unhappy, that I was from that time more unsettled than ever.

A short time after, a thought came into my head to dress myself in men's apparel, and set off by myself; but where to go, I did not know, nor what I was to do when I was gone. I had no thought what was to become of me, or what sorrow and anxiety I should bring upon my aged father and mother by losing me; but my inclinations were still bent on leaving home.

In order to do this, I went one day into my master's brother's room, and there found an old frock, an old pair of breeches, an old pair of pumps, and an old pair of stockings, all which did very well; but still was at a great loss for a hat; but then I recollected that my father had got one at home, if I could but procure it unknown to my parents; I therefore intended to get it without their knowledge; whereupon I went to my mother's house to ask her for a gown which I had given her the day before to mend for me. She answered, I should have it tomorrow. But little did my poor mother know what I wanted; for I went immediately into my father's room, took the hat, put it under my apron, and came downstairs; but I never said goodbye, or any thing else to my mother; but went home to my place, and packed up the things that I had got; and now only waited an opportunity to decamp.

On the first day of May, 1759, about six o'clock in the morning, I set off; and when I had got out of town into the fields, I pulled off my cloaths, and put on men's, leaving my own in a hedge, some in one place and some in another. Having thus dressed myself in men's habit, I went on to a place called Wingham, where a fair was held that day. Here I wandered about till evening; then went to a public house, and asked them to let me have a lodging that night, for which I agreed to give two-pence: now all the money I had when I came away was no more than five-pence. Accordingly I went to bed, and slept very well till morning, when I got up, and began to think which way I should go, as my money was so short; however, I proceeded towards Canterbury.

But as I was coming along upon the road, a post-chaise overtook me: I got up behind it, and rode to Canterbury; and then the post-chaise stopping, I quitted it, and walked on before, that they might not take any notice of me. After perceiving they did not take the horses out of the chaise, I concluded they were going farther, but did not know where; nor indeed did I care what became of me. When they came on the road to Chatham, I got up behind; not knowing whither I was going, never having been so far from home in my life.

When the chaise had reached Chatham, I got down, but was an utter stranger to the place; only I remembered to have heard my father and mother talk about a man's being hung in chains at Chatham; and, when I saw him, I thought this must be the place. I immediately began to think what I must do for a lodging; having no more than one penny, with which I went and bought some bread and cheese. Here I was quite at a loss what step to take: to go home again, was death to me; and to ask for a lodging, I was ashamed: so I walked up and down the streets, as it was the fair time, and sauntered about till it was dark.

As I stood considering what I should do, I looked about me, and saw a farm-house on the left hand of Chatham, as you go down the hill; I thought within myself I would go to it, and ask them to let me lie there; but when I came down to the house, I was ashamed to make the request. In this distressed situation I continued some time, not knowing how to proceed; for money I had none, and lie in the streets I never was used to, and what to do I did not know: but at last I resolved to lie in the straw, concluding that to be somewhat better than lying in the street; accordingly I went and got in among the straw, and laid myself down, but was so greatly terrified, that I was afraid to move; for when the pigs stirred a little, I thought somebody was coming to frighten me; therefore I did not dare open my eyes, lest I should see something frightful. I had but very little sleep; and when it was morning, I got up and shook my cloaths, and looked about to see if anybody perceived me get out. I then came down to the town, and went up to some men that belonged to a collier, who gave me some victuals and drink with them.

While I was standing here, a gentleman came up to me, and asked me if I would go to sea? "for," said he, "it is fine weather now at sea; and if you will go, I will get you a good master on board the *Sandwich*."

I replied, "Yes, Sir."

He then shewed me the nearest way on board; but instead of going to St. Princess's Bridge, (as the gentleman had directed me) I went over where the tide came up, being half up my legs in mud; but at length I got up to the bridge, and seeing a boat there, I asked the men belonging to it, if they were going on board the *Sandwich?* They told me they were; and asked me if I wanted to go on board? I told them, "Yes." They enquired who I wanted there? I told them, The gunner. They laughed, said I was a brave boy, and that I would do very well for him. But I did not know who was to be my master, or what I was to do, or whether I had strength to perform it: They then carried me on board.

When I came alongside the *Sandwich*, there were lighters with rigging or something belonging to her: that appeared all strange to me, as I never had seen such a large ship before; having often seen the hoys at Sandwich haven. When getting out of the lighter into the *Sandwich*, I thought it was impossible for such a great ship to go to sea. But what the men most took notice of, was, my observing how many windows the ship had got; she not yet having got her guns on board, for her ports were open.

When I found that the men laughed at me, I was angry with myself, for saying anything before I was acquainted with it. The sailors asked me if I would go to the gunner, who was in his cabin in the gun-room. Accordingly I went down: but it was remarkable I did not then know the head of the ship from the stern; for when I was down I could not find the way up again. When the gunner saw me, he asked where I came from, and how I came there? I told him, I had left my friends. He enquired if I had been 'prentice to anybody, and run away? I told him, "No."

"Well," said he, "should you like to go to sea?"

I replied, "Yes, Sir."

He then asked if I was hungry? I answered in the affirmative; having had but very little all the day. Upon this, he ordered his servant to serve me some biscuit and cheese. The boy went and brought me some, and said, "Here countryman, eat heartily"; which I accordingly did: for the biscuit being new, I liked it well, or rise my being hungry made it go down very sweet and savoury. After I had eat sufficiently, the gunner came and asked my name. I told him my name was William Chandler: but God knows how that came into my head; though it is true, my mother's maiden name was Chandler, and my fathers name William Lacy; therefore I took the name of Chandler.

Then the gunner told his boy to give me some victuals with him; and that when he went on shore, I was to go with him, (Jeremiah Pane, for that was his name) and we agreed very well: for he used to carry the people over the river, which sometimes put a few pence in his pocket; so that he always had some money, and was very good to me, and often gave me some, with which we sometimes tossed up for pies: therefore I lived very happy, considering the condition and situation I was in at that time.

There was another circumstance that attended me; for though I could not play the rogue much at first, yet in a little time afterwards I learned to do it very completely. But not knowing all this time who was my master, made me dissatisfied; for I had no linen to clean myself with, having only the shift that I had when I came from Ash; and I was very much afraid my fellow-servant should see my shirt had no collar; and besides, I had no other cloaths to wear but those I had on, which gave me such concern, that I often wished I was at home again. But the thoughts of seeing the young man again when I went home, diverted me entirely from that resolution, and made me conclude, that I had rather live upon bread and water, and go through all the trouble that I had brought, or might hereafter bring upon myself, than go home again.

I had been on board the *Sandwich* about four days when the carpenter came on board; and he had only one servant, who was at work in Chatham Yard; so at that time he had none on board. Now the gunner, whose name was Rd. Ruffel, liked me very well: he lived in lodgings at a place called Brompton, near Chatham; and the landlady of the house where he lodged had a son, who wanted to go to sea; and this woman was willing, if the gunner would take him, that he should go: whereupon the gunner and she agreed that he should go to sea with him as his servant. He told me, the carpenter would be glad to have me as his servant, for he was not willing I should be the captain's servant, that being the worst place in the ship, but at that time I did not know which was the best or worst: Mr. Ruffel, the gunner, therefore spoke to Mr. Richard Baker, the carpenter, for me. I was then sent for to the carpenter's cabin. He asked me, Whether I had been an apprentice to anybody, and was run away? I told him, "No."

"Well," said he, "are you a Kentish boy, or a boy of Kent?"

For my part, I did not then know the difference between a Kentish boy and a boy of Kent; but I answered, "A boy of Kent," which happened to be right. This made him laugh at me; for he was a merry man; but when out of humour, it was trouble enough to please him.

I shall here take occasion to relate what my master said to me concerning being his servant. There were two gentlemen with him. He first of all ordered me to fetch him a can of beer: I accordingly went, and brought it to him.

"Now," said he, "you must learn to make a can of flip, and to broil me a beefsteak, and to make my bed against I come to live on board. Come," said he, "and I will show you how to make my bed."

So we went to his cabin, in which there was a bed that turned up, and he began to take the bedcloaths off one by one.

"Now," said he, "you must shake them one by one, you must tumble and shake the bed about, then you must lay the sheets on one at a time, and lastly the blankets."

I replied, "Yes, Sir."

"Well," said he, "you will soon learn to make a bed, that I see already."

But he little knew who he had got to make his bed; and he not having any suspicion of my being a woman, I affected to appear as ignorant of the matter as if I had known nothing about it. He then provided for me a bed and bedding of a boatswain who came on board to see him, and then directed his mate to sling it up for me. When I attempted to get into bed at night, I got in at one side, and fell out on the other, which made all the seamen laugh at me; but, at it happened, there were not a great many on board, for being a new ship, but few had entered on board of her; so that my hammock was hung up in the sun-deck: but when the whole ship's company was on board, it was then taken down, and placed below in the wing where the carpenter and the yeomen both were; now it was better for me to lay there than anywhere else.

But I was very uneasy by lying there, on account of a quartermaster that lay in that place, whom I did not much like: and when I came to lie in the blankets, I did not know what to do, for I thought

I was eat up with vermin, having been on board ten days, and had no cloaths to shift myself with; so that I looked black enough to frighten anybody.

One day my master came on board, which was on a Saturday, and called me to go along with him; he had me up on the gangway, and shewed me three haystacks, and asked me if I saw them. I told him, "Yes, Sir."

"Well," said he, "I would have you come on shore tomorrow morning, in the first boat that you can get: walk till you have lost sight of those haystacks, and then enquire for one Mr. Baker, at St. Margaret's Bank, Chatham; and when you come to my house, you shall clean yourself." after which, my master went on shore; and I immediately thought that I had a great many particulars to remember; for fear therefore I should forget them, (as I could write well enough for myself to understand) I went to my pantry door, and there I set it down.

When the morning was come, I got up, and took the direction off the door, set it down on my hat, got on shore as soon as I could, and made all possible haste to rind out my master's house, and walked till I had lost sight of the haystacks. Seeing a woman stand at the door, I asked her where one Mr. Baker, carpenter of the *Sandwich* lived? She shewed me the house: and when I was got there, how glad was I! For I longed to see my mistress, and what sort of a house they lived in. I went and knocked, and there came a woman to the door, of whom I enquired, if one Mr. Baker lived there? Whereupon she fell a laughing, and said, "What do you want with him?"

I told her, my master had ordered me to come to him. Then she laughed again, and asked me if I knew my master when I saw him? I answered, "Yes."

She then bid me come in. I went into the kitchen where my master was sitting. My mistress asked me if that was my master? I replied "Yes, ma'am."

My master next enquired if I was hungry? Indeed I thought I could gladly eat a bit of bread and butter, and drink a bason of tea, for I even longed for some, having had none since I came away from Ash. But I told him, I was not hungry; notwithstanding which, he being a merry man, said to me, "You can eat a little bit?"

I answered, "Yes, Sir." On my saying this, my mistress gave me a bason of tea, and a bit of bread and butter, more than I could eat; but I quickly found out a way to dispose of the remainder, for what I could not eat, I put in my pocket.

When I had eaten my breakfast, my master called me out backwards, where there was some soap and water to wash myself with. How glad was I! Hardly being able to contain myself for joy. But there was something that gave me greater pleasure; for after I had washed myself, my mistress gave me a clean shirt, a pair of stockings, a pair of shoes, a coat and waistcoat, a checked handkerchief, and a red nightcap for me to wear at sea: I was also to have my hair cut off when I went on board; but this operation I did not like at all, yet was afraid to say anything to my master about it. However, I was very glad to find I had got clean cloaths to dress myself in, not having had that refreshment since I left Ash.

I must next inform you what trouble I was in; for I was afraid that my master would want to see my shirt; but my fears were soon over; for he only ordered me to put up all my cloaths together, and carry them on board with me. Now if I had changed my linen at his house, he would have seen my shift, and then he would have easily discovered my sex. Accordingly I took my things, went on board, and cleaned myself from top to toe. My master told me that I must wash my things every Monday, and that he would look them over every week; and, said he, "if I don't find them clean, I shall flog you."

Still I was in great trouble, lest he should ask me for my white shirt, for I had never a one to screen me from telling a lie; but I knew that Jeremiah Pane had got one; so I went and asked him if he would sell me his shirt; for it was not worth a great deal. "Well," said he, "you shall have it for nine-pence."

I replied, "I will give you nine-pence for it."

He agreed; I paid him the money, and got the shirt, to my no small joy. I then went and washed it, and carried it to my locker, for fear my master should ask me about it.

The ship had now orders to sail to Black Stakes, to take in her guns; consequently we proceeded to get them in. When I came to see the guns, I thought it was impossible for the ship to carry them, they being so large; for I had never seen a man-of-war before; so that it seemed very strange to me. But we had not lain long at Black Stakes before we went to the Nore, and there we lay till farther orders. We had now got a great number of men on board; some we had from the *Polly Green*, some from one ship, and some from another. These men were paid off from their several ships to come on board with us. But while we lay at the Nore, there came a bomb boat woman on board us, to sell all sorts of goods; this woman being an acquaintance of my masters, she had the use of his cabin; therefore I was desired to boil the tea kettle for her, and to do any thing she ordered me; and I was glad of it, for she was very good to me, and gave me a new purse to put my money in.

Now my master kept the key of the round-house; therefore the women had no convenient place of easing the necessity of nature; and he told me not to let them have the key, unless they gave me something; by this means I got several pence from them. My master then told me that my mistress was coming on board, and intended to stay all night, and desired me not to go from the cabin door, lest she should want me. Agreeable to my instructions, I sat down by the cabin door, and ran and fetched every thing that she had occasion for, but when I carried her any thing, instead of pulling off my hat, I was ready to make a curtsy, however, they did not take any notice of me. In general, I pleased her very well, never having any disagreement with one another.

It being now the last time that my mistress was to be on board, my master asked permission to go on shore, to take leave of all his friends and acquaintance; for we did not know how soon we might sail; and when we were out at sea, none of us knew that we might live to return again. My master and mistress therefore went on shore, and determined to take me with them; and I was very proud to think that I was to go with them to Chatham. We went all on shore, and had a supper dressed at the sign of the Sun: and when we broke up, my master and mistress went home, and I went along with them, and lay at their house. In the morning, I got up, eat my breakfast, and did what my mistress desired me: after she had breakfasted, we went and bought two check shirts and a pair of shoes for me to carry to sea, which occasioned me to think that I was well furnished, as I had four shirts and other necessities; therefore I thought that I was a sailor every inch of me.

When my mistress and I came home, we shewed my master what we had bought; he told me I should have a box made to put my cloaths in, and gave me a strict charge to take care of them; "for," he said, "when I came on board, they would steal the teeth out of my head if they could." I promised I would be as careful as possible of them. "Well," said he, "I hope you will; then told me we must go on board that evening"; and added, "I shall look at your cloaths, to see how clean you have kept them"; which last expression gave me a great deal of uneasiness, through fear of a discovery. My master and mistress parted after this, and we went on board; for we could not tell how soon the ship might sail.

After I was got on board, I began to think where I was going; for neither my father or mother knew where I was all this while, nor what was become of me; therefore my thoughts began to trouble me exceedingly, as I did not know whether I should live to come home again, or should ever see my disconsolate father and mother any more. These considerations occasioned me to reflect what sorrow and grief I had brought on my aged parents, who no doubt were very unhappy in having lost me so long. But seeing I had brought this misfortune on myself, I formed a resolution to go through with it, and suffer the consequences: for my mind suggested to me, that when I was out at sea, I could not run away; and if they discovered that I was a woman, I concluded it would be utterly impossible for me to escape. The serious reflection of these circumstances so aggravated the disquietude of my mind, that I did not know what to do: but I was the sole cause of all this perplexity myself.

I shall here take an opportunity of advising all maidens, never to give their minds to frequent the company of young men, or to seem fond of them: and I would also caution them, not to addict themselves to dancing with the male sex, as I wantonly did. But had I been in bed and asleep, which I ought to have been, the unknown sorrows I have since felt and experienced, would not have befallen me: but then I was young and foolish, and had not the thought or care of an older person. I would likewise admonish all young men, to beware how they marry; for I have seen so much of my own sex, that it is enough for a man to hate them; however, there are good and bad of both sexes.

I shall now proceed to relate some farther instances of my folly. In the first place, I thought, were I at home, I should be very happy if I could only see the young man again that I came away for; but a little recollection convinced me, it was in vain to think about that, as I could not run away; so by degrees this notion wore off, and I became quite contented: but when my master spoke angry, I used to sit down and cry for hours together. One day he told me I must go on shore with him at Sheerness, and take the little hand-basket with me, to bring spinach on board: so we went on shore, and the wind blew fresh. We did not stay long, but soon came on board again; which I was very desirous of, it being more agreeable to me to be on board than elsewhere.

After this, my master began to teach me the nature of the ship, and how to cook for him, which gave me an opportunity of discovering his natural temper. Sometimes, on mere trifling occasions, he was very hot, when things were not done according to his mind; on that account I was always afraid of him, and generally (when he was in a passion) stood with the cabin door in my hand, in order to make escape; which when I did, he always beat me. This usage I could hardly brook, especially as I knew that I was as real a woman as his mother. Besides, when at home, I could not bear to be spoke to, much less to have my faults told me. But now I found it was come to blows; and thought it was very hard to be struck by a man; which occasioned me to reflect that there was a wide difference between being at home, and in my present situation abroad.

About this time, orders came for us to sail immediately, to join the fleet at Brest, which put me under the most terrible apprehensions of coming to anchor in the Downs, lest I should see somebody there that knew me, being so near home. But it happened according to my wishes, since we did not anchor there; for having a fair wind, we sailed through the channel, and soon found the ship was too light for want of ballast. However, we quickly joined the fleet at Brest, and the captain of the *Sandwich*, with Admiral Geary, came on board us, and took the command of her, who hoisted his flag at the mizzen. With the admiral, came all his followers, both men and boys; and our hands were all turned over to the *Resolution*. We had now our full complement, which was 100. But among the admiral's servants, there were a great number of stout boys, very wicked and mischievous, and quite different in temper and behaviour from those of ours, who were sent from the Marine Society by Justice Fielding.

I never was under the least apprehension of these marine boys offering to molest or fight me; but those sturdy boys belonging to the admiral, were every now and then trying to pick a quarrel with me, nor was it long before they found means to put their design in execution; for one day being sent down in the galley to broil a beefsteak, one of these audacious boys, whose name William Severy, came and gave me such a slap in the face that made me reel.

This insult brought a little choler on me, which by repeated affronts almost grew into fury. I considered it would only make me sick if I could not beat him; and also reflected that my cause was just, for I never had attempted to anger him, though he was perpetually using me ill. From these considerations, on his next abuse, I was determined to try the event. Lieutenant Cook knowing me better than any of them, and at the same time being sensible that I had given no just cause for these proceedings, told me I should fight him, and if conqueror, should have a plum pudding, and that he would in the meantime mind the steak. Upon which, I went aft to the main hatchway, and pulled off my jacket; but they wanted me to pull off my shirt, which I would not suffer, for fear of being discovered that I was a woman, and it was with much difficulty that I could keep it on.

Hereupon we instantly engaged, and fought a great while; but, during the combat, he threw me such violent cross buttocks, that were almost enough to dash my brains out; but I never gave out, for I knew if I did, I should have one or other of them continually upon me: therefore we kept to it with great obstinacy on both sides; and I soon began to get the advantage of my antagonist, which all the people who knew me perceiving, seemed greatly pleased, especially when he declined fighting any more; and the more so, as he was looked upon as the best fighter among them.

This contest ending so favourably for me, I reigned mister over the rest, they being all afraid of me: and it was a most lucky circumstance, that I had spirit and vigour to conquer him who was my greatest adversary; for if I had not, I should have been so harassed and ill-treated amongst them, that my very life would have been a burden. However, all the time I was fighting, my master knew nothing of the matter; but, when over, somebody told him. As soon as I had put myself in some tolerable order, I went for the steak, and I carried it to his cabin, being a little afraid that I should be chastised.

"Well," said he, "you have been a long while about the steak, I hope it is well done now?"

"Yes, Sir," said I.

"Why," says he, looking very attentively, "I suppose you have been fighting?"

I answered, "Yes, Sir, I was forced to fight, or else be drubbed."

"But," said he, "I hope you have not been beat?"

I replied, "No, Sir."

"Well," said he, "when you fight again, let me know, and I will be bound you shall beat them;" so that, upon the whole, I came off with flying colours. From this time, the boy and I who fought, became as well reconciled to one another as if we had been brothers; and he always let me share part of what he had.

It was now more than two months since I had left my father and mother, who had never heard of me; about which time, we received orders for the *Resolution* to sail for England, to be repaired. I observed the people now on board were employing themselves in writing letters to their friends; which put a thought into my head to write to my mother, to inform her where I was, which I knew would be a great satisfaction to my parents. I could write but very indifferently; and to entrust any person with my thoughts on this occasion, I imagined would be very improper. At last, I resolved to write myself; but, after having wrote my letter, I had nothing to seal it with, and, thinking a bit of pitch would do, I went to the pitch-tub for some, which when I thought I had got, it proved to be tar, so that with using it I soiled the letter very much. I was now greatly perplexed to contrive a method to seal it up. At length, one of the men, who observed I had been writing, gave me a wafer, which did completely. Soon after this, the boat came on board, and took away all the letters, and mine with the rest; the contents of which I now present you with, and are as follows:—

July 3, 1759.
Hond. Father and Mother,
This comes with my duty to you, and hope that you are both in good health, as I am at present, thanks be to God for it. I would have you make yourselves as easy as you can, for I have got a very good master, who is carpenter on board the *Sandwich*; and am now upon the French coast, right over Brest: shall be glad to hear from you as soon as you can. So no more at present, from Your undutiful daughter,

Mary Lacy.
P.S. Please to direct thus, For William Chandler, on board the *Sandwich*, at Brest.

These were the contents of the letter I sent to my father and mother, to acquaint them where I was; and occasion to the reflection, that children too often grieve and distress their parents by rash and disobedient behaviour; and many, alas! bring sorrow and trouble upon their heads, at the very period of life it behoves them rather to add to their comfort and joy, by all the means in their power.

In about six weeks after, while we lay at Brest, I received a letter from my father and mother. When the men called and told me there was a letter for me, I immediately ran for joy to think that I got an answer sent me; but, nevertheless, was afraid to open it, lest I should find therein a severe rebuke for running away; however, at last, (with some reluctance) I broke it open, and, to my great pleasure an satisfaction, found it contained as follows:—

Ash, Aug. 16, 1759.

My dear Child,

I received yours safe, and was glad to hear that you are in good health; but I have been at death's door almost with grief for you. Your cloaths, after your departure, were found in a hedge, which occasioned me to think you were murdered; therefore I have had no rest day or night; for I thought, that if you had been alive, you would have writ to me before. However, as you have writ to me now, I shall make myself as easy as I can; but shall still have hopes of seeing you again. And I hope you will put your trust in God, and beg that he will help you in all your difficulties and trials. When you have an opportunity to write to me, don't be neglectful; and may the blessing of God be with you! So no more at present, from

Your afflicted Father and Mother,

Wm. and Mary Lacy!'

After I had read the letter, I could not help crying, to think what trouble and sorrow I had brought on my parents; and on considering that I should be the cause of bringing aged hairs with sorrow to the grave, perhaps much sooner than might otherwise have happened. I must therefore here address myself to all undutiful children, hoping they will mind what I say, and be attentive to the instructions and advice of their parents in their youthful days, whereby they may escape many dangers and miseries that a forward and stubborn conduct will bring upon them.

Whilst I was reading my letter, one of the boys went and told my master that I was crying; on his observing which, he asked me what I cried for, and if any body had abused me? I answered, "No, Sir."

"What is the cause then?" said he "I beg you will tell me."

I then gave him to understand I had received a letter from my father and mother.

"Well," said he, "are they dead or alive?"

I told him, they were alive and well; but that I was afraid they would chide me for running away. He observed, "I like you the better for remembering your parents; and God will love all them who love their parents."

On hearing him express himself thus, I thought God was very merciful to me, in directing me to such a good master: for if he beat me himself, he would not suffer anybody else to do so: besides, I knew his temper so well, that nobody else could please him like myself, which indeed I sometimes found it very difficult to do; for if anything went contrary to his mind, and made him angry, he would be sure to vent it on somebody or other. Upon the whole, it was a hard matter to please him; for he would on some occasions fall into such violent passions, that he neither knew what he said or did.

He frequently accustomed himself to sit up late, either with the gunner or boatswain; who, when they all met together, would continue in each other's company during the whole night, which obliged me to be up very late on my master's account; and have frequently been kept so long from my rest till I have been stiff and almost dead with cold. When in liquor, he used to make me many fair promises; and, amongst others, that he would put me 'prentice, and find me with all my cloaths during the time; and that I should have my money to send home to my parents.

After talking to me in this manner, he would add, "William, you are a good boy; and though I scold you sometimes, it is only because you don't do as I desire you: however, you are a good boy in the main, too. I must also tell you, William, that your mistress is a very good woman: but, do you hear me? Don't tell her that I say so, or that I sit up late at night. She will ask you a great many questions about me, and what company I keep, but be sure not to inform her."

It may not be improper to observe here, that of all the officers' boys in the ship, the boatswain's was the least serviceable of any, inasmuch as he could not even boil the kettle for his master's breakfast; so that I used to do that and other things for him. The boatswain, I must own, was very good to me for it; as he gave me a pair of stockings, and several other necessaries, which made me take delight to wait on him: and my master told me, that I might go to his cabin when I pleased. But this good fortune did not last long; for, he being ordered away from our ship, I lost a good friend; after which, I had reason to apply the proverb to my own case, which says, "*When the old one is gone, there seldom comes a better;*" as he was, through his obliging behaviour, beloved by the whole ship's company. He was succeeded by a boatswain taken from the *Somerset* man-of-war.

A few days after, as gunner and boatswain's boy were sitting down to dinner, and myself standing (being always in a hurry, and indifferent whether I stood or sat) my master observing from his cabin that the boatswain's boy was sitting while I was standing near him, immediately ordered me to make him rise, and take his seat. For my part, I did not desire to do any such thing, as I imagined it would have been looked upon as a very great breach of good manners to disturb any person so roughly.

Another time the lieutenant told me to put a hand to the staysail braces, and help to hale them up. My master seeing this, called to me, and asked what I was doing? I told him the lieutenant ordered me to do it. He replied, "You have no business to do any such work; nor," added he, "shall a servant of mine do any thing of that nature;" and cautioned me to remember, that I did not come to be their servant, but his.

As we lay still at Brest, some men were draughted from the *Temple* to come on board us: amongst them was a young man that I knew at Ash, whose name was Henry Hambrook; and I was much afraid he would know me. However, having been on board for some time, he one day came and asked, if I did not come from Ash? Not being willing to know him, I enquired what reason he had for asking such a question? "Oh," said he, "I thought I knew you."

However, I took no farther notice of what he said concerning me: nor did he mention the matter again to any other person, to my knowledge, though he well knew who I was.

Soon after this, I was taken with the rheumatism in my fingers, which occasioned them to swell very much: not knowing the cause, I went and shewed them to my master. "Let me see your fingers," said he, and fell a laughing at me, adding, "hang me if William is not growing rich: You dog, you have got the gout in your fingers." This passed on a day or two, when I was seized with it in my legs, and was so bad that I could not walk. My master was then at a loss what to do with me; but thought proper to send down for the doctor to come and look at me. He told me, that I must go down into the bay in the sick birth. Well knowing what a nasty unwholesome place it was, the very thoughts of going thither made me very uneasy; nevertheless, I did not choose to say anything to my master about it. I was accordingly carried down; but he sent me thither every day some tea and biscuit buttered for breakfast. This I received from the hands of an old man, who was of so uncleanly a disposition, that had I been ever so well, I could not have relished it from him. I remained in this disagreeable place for several weeks; but, growing worse and worse, was much altered.

While in this disagreeable situation, the young man above-mentioned frequently came down to see me; but never took any notice that he knew me. Thinking therefore, that he came out of friendship, I desired him to tell my master that I should be glad he would move me to some other part of the ship, for if he did not, it would soon be the death of me. He immediately went and related all I had said to him. Whereupon my master came down to see me; when I told him as before, that I should soon die if not removed from thence.

"Well," said he, "you shall come up and sit in my cabin." And indeed very glad I was to think I should be taken out of that loathsome place. He then sent two men to bring me into his cabin, and ordered the yeoman to warm some water to wash my hands and face, which he cleaned and wiped himself; and took as much care of me as if I had been one of this own, which he evidenced by many instances of his goodness towards me.

I was unable to sit up in the cabin the whole day, and at night was carried down. Next morning, when the doctor called to visit the sick, he asked me how I did? I answered, "Very bad." He then began to be very angry that I went up to my master's cabin and told me, I should not go there any more till I was better. Upon which, I fell a crying, which I could not help, on thinking I must be confined below. In order to prevent, if possible, this disagreeable circumstance, I desired the man to acquaint my master what the doctor had said. In consequence of which, my master went down to the doctor, and told him roundly, that I should come up every day to his cabin, for my staying there was the readiest way to kill me.

Accordingly I was allowed to come up every day as before; by which means I soon became better. But being still very weak, my master got me crutches, with a spike at each end, for my safety to walk about on the deck; and, when anybody affronted me in an ill-natured way, I used to throw my crutch at them. The care I was constantly taken of by the person under whom Providence had placed me was such, that he would not suffer me to wait on him, lest I should catch cold again; so that by this precaution I soon recovered my health and strength.

In a short time after, we received orders to sail to Plymouth, to take in ballast and more provision, and afterwards to join the fleet again at Brest. When we were returned, Admiral Hawke made a signal for all the fleet to clear ship, which we did for three or four days; expecting the French fleet out every hour. But finding they made no preparation to leave the harbour, we put up all the officers cabins; and, on the 10th of November 1759, being His Majesty's birthday, the admiral made a signal for all the ships to fire the same number of guns as in England on this occasion. We ran in as near the French coast as we could; after which, the admiral began to fire: and after having fired all round, we all tacked about, and stood off from the land; yet did not stand far off, but lay to, to see if the enemy would venture out. It seemed as if they thought we were going to land at Brest, or some other place; for in the night they made bonfires all round the country, to alarm and give notice to their people, that we were about to land. But when the wind was fair for us to stand off from the shore, it was favourable for them to sail. Soon after, it blowing hard, and from a proper point for us to quit the French coast, the admiral made a signal for all the fleet to anchor in Torbay; which we accordingly did.

During the time the *Sandwich* lay in the foresaid bay, orders came for us to sail to Plymouth. But while we were under way, there came a ship acquainting the admiral that the French fleet had got out, and were directing their course towards the West Indies. Immediately upon this intelligence, some of our ships cut their cables, others weighed their anchors, and we soon came up with them at Quiberon Bay, where we began the engagement, and soon forced them to surrender; for some sheered off, others were taken, and several of them threw their guns overboard: So after dispersing and destroying the best fleet they had, we imagined the war would soon be at an end. However, our ship had no share in the battle, for we were at that time in Plymouth; but soon received orders to go to Quiberon Bay, to watch the motions of the French there. Hereupon we sailed, and anchored in the bay; and had a great deal of pleasure in viewing the country, as we were stationed there some time.

My master now asked me how I liked the sea? I replied, I liked it very well. "But," said he, "should you not be afraid if you were to come to an engagement?"

I answered, "No; for I should have work enough to fetch powder to the gun I was quartered at, therefore should have no time to think of that."

He then told me, I should not be able to bring the powder fast enough. I replied, "I'll take it from the little boys, and cause them to fetch more, before the gun shall want powder;" at which he laughed heartily, to hear me talk so, as he well might.

We continued here for some time; and were afterwards ordered to the Bay of Biscay. I must here observe, that a person, who is a stranger to these great and boisterous seas, would think it impossible for a large ship to ride in them: but I slept many months on the ocean, where I have been tossed up and down at an amazing rate. As we were stationed off Cape Finisterre, and the wind blowing so hard that we could not lie there, we afterwards went and anchored in Quiberon Bay, and when there, the officers went frequently on shore; which our master perceiving, obtained leave for me to go with the admiral's boys when an opportunity offered.

About this time, the princess' boat went on shore, accompanied by all the band of music; and we had a great deal of pleasure in walking about the island in the day time; but there were very few people in it. When they saw our boat coming on shore, they sent the young women out of the island, for fear of our officers; and there were left remaining only two or three old men, and one old woman. We here found very fine grapes, and other sort of fruits; but our officers would not allow us to take any of their fruits, except grapes; and if we had an inclination for any others, we were obliged to pay for them. I saw no other habitations than two or three old huts which they lived in.

In the evening we went on board; when my master asked me how I liked the island? I told him, I liked it very well, and that I thought it was a very pleasant place; but imagined it must be extremely cold in winter. Notwithstanding this agreeableness of his temper at intervals, it was in general a difficult matter to please him; for sometimes, after providing one thing for his breakfast, he would require another; for instance, when I had made sage tea, he would have gruel; and, after green, he would order *bohea* to be made, with biscuit split, toasted and buttered; and if either of these things were prepared in any respect displeasing to him, he would fling it at me, though not with any real intention of hurting me; nay, the very cups and saucers would not escape his violent passion: so that I was afraid of getting ready his breakfast lest he should flog me, and then I should run the utmost risk of being discovered.

On this account I was always upon my guard as much as possible. One time when I did not get his breakfast to please him, he told me I should be flogged at the gun for my neglect; and being afraid he would do it, I sat down and cried all the time the gunner and he were at breakfast. My master afterwards said to the gunner, "Don't you think now that William ought to be flogged for not getting the breakfast better?"

But the gunner being always a good friend to me, said, "I will be bound for William this time that he will do so no more"

"What!" returned my master, "will you, who have been bound so often for him, be answerable again for his good behaviour? If so, for this time I'll take your word; but remember, the next time he does any thing amiss, I will send for you, and then you shall be flogged for him."

By this means I got off scot free. He would sometimes kick me with such violence, as if he would force me through the cabin; and when he had the gout, would be so peevish and passionate, that I found it extremely troublesome and difficult to please him, insomuch that I often wished him dead.

My master once told me, he should come and look in my locker again, to see what things I had there. Accordingly he came; and on examining it, he missed the blacking bottle, in which I used to make his blacking. Knowing it was broke, I stood off for fear, as I knew I should expose myself to his resentment. He asked me, "Where is the blacking bottle?"

I answered, "Sir, it is broke."

He then fell into a great passion. "You dog, said he, I will have you flogged for it; I thought my shoes did not shine as they used to do"

However, I happily escaped the flogging at this time. He always caused me clean my own shoes as well as those that belonged to him; and if they were not done to his mind, he would kick me with great violence. Whereupon he peremptorily expressed himself thus, "You dog, I will make you go neat and clean; for you are a carpenter's servant, and you shall appear as such."

Not long after this circumstance, my master was seized with another severe fit of the gout, which increased to such a degree, that I was obliged to sew some flannel upon his legs; and if I did not do it to please him, I was sure to be severely reprimanded; and he was withal so troublesome, that if I was but just lain down in my hammock, he would send somebody to fetch me up; therefore I had but little rest at a time, as he was always wanting something. If I was gone only a minute from the cabin door, he would pass the word fore and aft for boy William, as he called me; so that I was forced to run, lest I should be chastised. But when everything went agreeable with him, he would then be apt to make me many fair promises; and, among others, that he would bind me out 'prentice, and clothe me during the time, though I could never believe it would come to anything.

At this time, there were the *Ramillies*, the *Royal William*, and five other ships with us; but on January 12, 1760, a dreadful hurricane arose, which lasted two days; by reason of this storm we lost sight of each other, not knowing where we were; and the sea running mountains high, all of us expected to perish. We had seven men drowned, had sprung our main and foremast, and were very nigh the land; but as it pleased God to give us a sight of the danger we were in, we very happily kept clear of the land, and next day went into Plymouth Sound, when my master went on shore into the yard to report the damage of the ship. I went with him; and we were greatly affected on seeing that only twenty-five men were saved out of 700 that were in the *Ramillies*, which was lost on the 14th of January, 1760.

On this melancholy occasion, I thought God was very good and merciful to us, that we escaped in that terrible tempest; notwithstanding which, we were no sooner delivered from the danger of the seas than we forgot it, and neglected to give God thanks for so great a mercy; but on the contrary, were still from one day to another running on in a greater course of wickedness than before.

I now thought that if I could but get clear of the ship, I should esteem myself very happy, but recollected I had no money; for my master had never paid me any; and my cloaths were made out of old canvas. When I was served with wine, I sold it for two shillings a bottle, and that helped to provide me some shirts; for I had very little money of my master.

At this time we received orders to go into the Hamoaze, to have our ship repaired, which I was glad of, as I always went on shore with my master, who frequented the sign of the Cross Keys at North Conner, kept by one Mr. P——s. He obtained leave to stay on shore, and gave me the like permission till he went on board. An unfortunate circumstance attended me here, which was, that I had a bedfellow allotted me, being obliged to lie with the post-chaise boy, which gave me great concern; however, it was the will of God I should not be discovered at that time, though I continued in this situation while the ship lay at Plymouth.

When my master was sober, he would sit down and reckon what money he had spent, the thoughts of which ruffled his temper greatly, and at such times I was always the chief object of his resentment; therefore I was sorry when he was not in liquor.

In a short time our ship was ready to go to sea again; then my master and the gunner went into the country to buy some fowls, pigs, ducks, and a great quantity of garden stuff, which were all carried on board. Being ready for sea, we were ordered to proceed to Rochelle and Basque Roads, and keep our station there till further orders. We had not been long at sea before my master was seized with such a severe fit of gout, that I thought he would have died before we could get home; therefore I heartily wished we were in England again. Besides, I had no peace day after day; and as he still grew worse and worse, I was quite tired of my life, having a great number of different kinds of messes continually to make for him.

One day as he was sitting in his cabin, he told me he heard we were going for England; and he seemed greatly pleased, as well as I, that the ship had received orders to sail for Portsmouth; because I thought he would then have liberty to go into sick quarters as soon as he could. When we came in sight of the Isle of Wight, my master began to pack up all his things to be ready to go on shore at Portsmouth; and on his arrival there, he wrote a letter to Chatham for my mistress to come down to him. It was not long before she came on board the *Sandwich*, where she lay all night, but was soon tired of the ship. Next day my mistress was conducted all over the cabin, when she asked my master several trivial questions concerning the time how long he had had this and the other convenience. To all which, he told her, it was as his master pleased; for when he was in a good humour he would call me so. She did not find fault with anything, but was soon tired of being on board, which I was not sorry for, because I thought I should then have a little time to myself.

My master having liberty to go on shore, took lodgings at one Mr. Allen's, a shipwright, where I accompanied him; and as a favourable opportunity offered itself, by the leisure time afforded me here, I resolved to embrace it, in order to write to my parents, which I did in the following terms:—

Portsmouth, Oct. 27, 1760

Hond. Father and Mother,

This comes with my duty to you, and hope these lines will find you in good health, as I am at present. I am very sorry that I ran away from you, and that I have been so neglectful in writing; but I beg leave to tell you, that I have no thoughts of coming to Ash again, but should be very glad to see you; however, in that I must trust to the will of God. Last January, in a storm of wind, we lost seven men. The *Ramillies* was lost at the same time, and only 25 men saved; but by the blessing of God it was not my lot. I am in some hopes I shall have a little money to send you,

when my master pays me; for I have received none yet. He talks of paying soon; so that you need not expect to hear from me till such time as I am able to send you what money I can spare. My kind love to my brother and sister, and all friends that know me. Shall be glad to hear from you as soon as you can conveniently write. So no more at present, from
Your undutiful Daughter,

Mary Lacy.

N.B. Please to direct thus, For William Chandler, on board the *Sandwich*, in Portsmouth harbour.

I shall now return to my master and mistress. Being on shore, one day he told me I must go on board with him next morning. We stayed in the ship that night; and in the morning he packed up some wine for me to carry on shore: But the wind blowing fresh, he would go in a cutter that was there; and not being able to reach the harbour, we were obliged to land at the south beach. Just upon our reaching the shore the cutter filled with water, which made us very wet; and from this unfortunate accident, I had the basket of wine to carry full two miles to Portsmouth Common, after having narrowly escaped with our lives. However, we got home in good time, though I was obliged to lie at a public house, the sign of the Ship and Castle.

In the morning I went down to my masters lodgings, and did the usual business; such as cleaning his room, and getting his breakfast ready. My mistress then began to enquire in what condition my cloaths were, and whether they wanted repair? My master told her, he had bought me a purser's jacket, but it was too big. Whereupon she ordered me to bring my things on shore when I went on board again, and she would teach me how to mend them. Accordingly I went on board, and brought them with me: and my mistress and I being alone, she began to ask how my master and I agreed? What time he went to bed, and what company he kept? I told her, the gunner and he, who both messed together, were very agreeable; that my master kept very regular hours, and went to bed in good time: for I took great care not to say anything that might cause a disagreement betwixt them. Nevertheless, she would often shift me from one thing to another; yet I still kept upon my guard: And telling her at last I knew nothing of the things she questioned me about, she left off importuning me.

Next day my mistress told me I must to the town-market with her, to buy something for Sunday's dinner. Taking the hand-basket with me, we went together; but had not gone far before we met with one or two of the sailors companions who knew me. They asked me how I did; and a little conversation passed betwixt us. My mistress did not stop to observe who they were, or what they did: but when I came up to her again, she asked me who they were? I told her what I knew of them. When we came to the market, my mistress was always upon the wing, going from one place to another, asking the price of several things, and at length she bought of those whose provisions she cheapened at first; and after having bought a duck, we went home to our lodgings.

As soon as my master came home, his wife began to tell him how many women had been enquiring after me.

"Well," said my master, "I suppose you have boiled the tea kettle for them?"

"Yes, Sir," said I, "I have," for I don't like to be ill-natured; if I had, I should have been beat very unmercifully ere now; but thank God I never had the ill will of any of them; and I believe if any of them had seen me ill used, they would have taken my part.

My master replied, "I would have you learn to be good natured to everybody, and not to practice any bad tricks."

I still continued on shore, and lay at the Ship and Castle; but went every day to wait on my mistress. At last the ship was ordered into dock, where my master set me to work, which was to saw some wood up, and bring it home to his lodgings; however, I was ordered to lie on board, and come on shore every morning, which I was very glad of, because I thought in that case nobody would interrupt me.

One day wanting to put on a clean shirt before I came from aboard, I found my shirts were all wet; notwithstanding which, I did not stop to dry the one I used, but very unadvisedly put it on as it was, and went on shore. I had not been long there till I was seized with the rheumatism to such a degree that I was carried on board; and next day grew so very ill, that the doctor told me I must go to the hospital.

At this time my master had procured a boat to carry his things from the ship to his lodgings; whereupon the doctor's mate asked my master if he would let him have the boat, with two or three hands to carry me to the hospital? To which he consented, and sent one J—n B—n, the carpenter's mate, and the doctor's mate, whose name was Mr. L—e. I was then carried up to the agent in the hospital, and he ordered me to be taken into the fifth ward south, where I was put to bed very bad, and grew worse and worse every day; and at length became so delirious, that I neither knew what I said, or to whom I spoke.

In this condition I remained till they thought it necessary to bleed me, by which I received great relief.

Being now grown a little better, I got up, but was not able to walk much; however, I recovered the use of my hands, and mended by degrees. When I was able to walk about the room, it came into my head, that I would try to go downstairs; and having got as far as the staircase, the wind blew so cold, that I thought it would cut me asunder; therefore I was obliged to go back again into my ward. The nurse asked me how far I had been? I told her, as far as the staircase; but felt it so very cold, that I could venture no farther. She then told me the danger I was in of catching cold again, which determined me not to attempt going again till the weather was finer.

While I continued here, the *Sandwich* sailed from Spithead to the Nore, with orders to go to Rochelle; but being sick, my master went and left me behind.

The weather now proving warmer, I endeavoured a second time to go downstairs. But when I came to the staircase, I found I was not able; for I could not bend my knees. I therefore sat down on the stairs, and slid from one step to the other till I got to the foot, which was very troublesome for me before I could effect it. I then went under one of the arches where the sun shone warmest.

Being now pretty well recovered, they sent me on board the *Royal Sovereign*, a guardship at Spithead, as a supernumerary man, which I was glad of; for soon after Admiral Geary and all his servants came on board, whom I knew; and they were glad to see me. There was one John Grant who had a woman on board with him, and one George Robinson, a quarter-master, both of whom invited me to mess with them. I was very glad of the offer; because I then thought I should have some tea, as there would be a woman in the company. The quartermaster was likewise very kind to me; for he always keep some tea and sugar partly on my account; and we often drank tea together.

I shall now return to my former relation concerning my being admitted into the mess, which I continued in for some time. The young woman and I were very intimate, and she was exceeding fond of me; so that we used to play together like young children, insomuch that our messmates believed we were too familiar together; but neither of us regarded their surmises; and if they said any thing to her, she told them that if anything like what they suspected had passed between us, the same should be practised in future. However, when John Grant became acquainted that she and I were so fond of each other's company, he began to be somewhat displeased; nevertheless, he was afraid to take any notice of it, lest his messmates should laugh at him; yet though he seemed to wink at it, he shewed her several tokens of this resentment, by beating her, and otherwise using her very ill, threatening to send her on shore.

Soon after this I received a letter from my parents, which gave me great pleasure, the contents of which are as follows:—

Ash, May 22, 1761.

Dear Child,

I received your letter very safe, and hope these few lines will find you in good health, as we are at present, thanks be to God for it. I would not have you believe that I thought it was too much trouble to write to you, since I am very glad to find you are in good health. But still, my dear child, when I think about you, it makes me almost distracted to reflect on your present situation, and the hardships you must needs go through. These thoughts, I say, make my heart ready to burst. However, I hope you will study to put your trust in God, who will help you in all your difficulties; and also flatter myself that I shall have the pleasure of seeing you some time or other. All friends send their kind love to you, wish you well out of all your troubles, and desire you will write as soon as convenient. Your brother and sister send their kind love to you. I shall now conclude with our parental affection and blessing, from

Your afflicted Father and Mother,

Wm. and Mary Lacy

When I had read the above letter, I again condemned myself for the sorrow I had brought on my parents, by running away from them, which I was the sole cause of; for if I had made them acquainted with my design, they in all probability would have prevented it. May these bad effects of my rash conduct serve as a caution to forward children to mind their parents in their youthful days, which may prove to them a means of escaping many dangers they may be exposed to; and thus, by obedient behaviour, they will bring comfort on their aged parents heads, instead of grief and affliction as I did.

I proceed now to farther instances of my folly. While I was standing one day on the deck, the boatswain's mate desired me to go down to the yeoman for a bucket. As I was going to the store-room, the men were scraping the side of the ship; the ports being open on one side and shut on the other, and the men drawing water out of the hold, I perceived I could not go down there; however, the gratings being open, I thought I would jump over the cable, the consequence of which imprudence was, I fell down the forehold with my head upon the chime of a cask, and cut a terrible wound in it, which laid it quite open.

When my messmates came down and beheld me, they were so frightened that they knew not what to do; however, they carried me into the cockpit to the doctor's mate, who bled and dressed my head, but was forced to sew it up with three stitches. During the time he did this, I was senseless; and when I came to myself, I was very apprehensive lest the doctor, in searching for bruises about my body, should discover that I was a woman; but it fortunately happened, he being a middle aged gentleman, was not very inquisitive; and my messmates being advanced in years, and not so active as young people, did not tumble me about to undress me.

As it was next to a miracle my sex was not discovered on the above occasion, I esteemed it a singular mercy God had prevented it at that time. The pain in my head, in consequence of the fall, was so exceedingly bad, that I was almost deprived of my senses; yet, notwithstanding my pain and illness, I had a continual fear upon me of being found out: and as I lay in my hammock, I was always listening to hear what they said, or whether they had made any discovery. My apprehensions were soon afterwards removed, on finding they were as ignorant as before, with respect to that particular; so that I continued in my hammock very easy and satisfied.

When one Mr. P—g—e, the doctor, came on board, he ordered my hammock to be lowered; and after dressing my head, he left me to the care of my messmates, who accordingly attended upon me.

There was at that time a bumboat woman on board, who gave me some tea and cake, and was otherwise very good to me. Her kindness was the more acceptable, as my teeth were grown so loose in my head, that I could not eat any thing; but by the care of this woman, I wanted for nothing; and in a short time found myself so much recovered, that I could go to the doctor, and have my head dressed every day. He often told me that he should give me the St. Andrews Cross, which made me afraid to go afterwards, lest he should cut me. However, as he perceived I was in a fair way of being cured, I escaped the operation.

Once on the doctor's mate dressing my head, he bound it up so very tight, that it ached prodigiously; and I was not able to bear it. For this reason I went to him myself, desired he would look at my head, and told him it pained me so much that I fiercely knew how to sustain it. His answer was, he could not open it. Whereupon I went away as I came: but in a little time after, I found myself obliged to go to the doctor again, and tell him, that if he would not open it, I must endeavour to find somebody else that would. After hearing me express myself in this peremptory manner, he began to look at my head, and by loosening the bandage, gave me great ease, and removed the excruciating pain which the tightness had occasioned.

I then went to bed, and was taken so ill of a fever, that I became senseless for three or four days. The doctor perceiving this, told my messmates he would have me conveyed to the hospital in the morning, if I grew no better. They replied, he should not send me there, alleging, it would be the only way to put a final period to my existence, if I was carried into the cold. But it pleased God to remove the fever in a short time; so next day when the doctor came, and found it had left me, he thought I should soon recover my wonted health and strength. During the time of the fever, the doctor's mate let me blood, as I found afterwards, by my garter upon the orifice, which put me in great fear, lest he had discovered my sex. But when he came next to see me, he did not mention a word concerning that, which I am sure he would, had he known I had been a woman.

I now grew better every day; and if I had had a friend, I could have procured a smart ticket for Chatham, and should have received four pounds a year, or something more: But I was at that time utterly ignorant of such a provision; and had nobody to advise or direct me about it, my master being gone to sea. But by the blessing of God, I was at last better provided for.

As soon as I was pretty well recovered, I went to work again; and in a short time was as well as ever. I was very sorry to find that my messmate George Robinson had left the ship, as I knew not what was become of him, nor have I heard of him since. This occasioned me to get a new messmate, which was the captain of the forecastle, whose name was Philip M—t—n, who had a notable woman to his wife. They were worth money, and lived very happy together on board the ship; and indeed few in our circumstances lived so comfortably as we did. This woman used to wash for me, and also for impressed men as they came on board; and if I did any work for these pressed men, my messmates would tell them they must pay me for it, because I had no friend in the world to help me: so that when I had done any thing for them, one would give me a pair of stockings, another breeches, and the rest would supply me in return with other necessaries; therefore I wanted for nothing of that sort.

The boatswain observing me so very tractable, by which I gained the good will of everybody, seemed desirous I should come and mess with him, which appeared very strange to me, because he never knew me before: however, I soon found out the cause, which was as follows: There being a quartermaster's wife on board that came from the Isle of Wight, who sold all manner of things; and being a particular acquaintance of the boatswains, she urged him to ask me to mess with him, in order to look after her things. But at that time I had an opportunity of doing something more serviceable for myself, than barely looking after their matters, which was, to go down into the school to learn to write and cast accompts.

Some time after this, having gone through a great deal of trouble, by serving different persons on board, my whole endeavour being always employed to please and assist every body as well as I could; at length, being induced by the boatswain's repeated acts of kindness to me, I came to a resolution of messing with him whenever he should hint the matter again, which he soon did: and indeed I afterwards found I had exchanged messmates to my own case and advantage. He being very kind to me, I lived extremely happy; for as he did not come on board above once or twice a week, I had but little else to do than make his bed, and dress him a bit of victuals; so that I had time enough to wait upon the women.

The boatswain's wife, who was a handsome woman, coming on board with her father and mother, I was ordered to dress some fish for them, which they were pleased to say were very well served up, and gave me sixpence as a gratuity for my trouble and care. He told me at the same time, that he would procure leave for me to go on shore from time to time; but I never had the good fortune to find that he performed this promise.

I had now been on board the *Royal Sovereign* one year and near seven months, when I received a letter from my master, which I here present to you, and is as follows:

> From on board the *Sandwich*, Basque Road.
> Oct. 2, 1762.

William

I have taken this opportunity to write to you, to let you know that very shortly we expect to come to Spithead, and then hope to hear a good account of you; which if I do, will perform my promise, to put you to 'prentice in Chatham Yard, it you like it. Give my compliments to Mr. Jennings, the carpenter on board your ship; and you may shew him this letter if you please. I would have you be good; and take great care of yourself. The last time I heard from your mistress, she was very well. Take no cloaths from the captain; if you do, I shall not get your wages. So no more at present, from

Yours, etc.

Rich. Baker.

This letter, according to my masters instructions, I shewed the carpenter and boatswain, who said my master promised very fair; and observed I had no reason to be afraid of having a bad name, for every body that knew my behaviour and conduct, would speak well of me. It gave me great pleasure to hear from my master; and when the *Sandwich* came, that the peace would be concluded.

Soon after this, the boatswain told me that all the ships were going into harbour to be paid off, and that the *Sovereign* would be the first; which induced me to think of engaging as an apprentice to my master at Chatham, though it did not entirely suit my inclination, because I knew there would be many persons at that place who were acquainted with me, and by that means I might soon be discovered: therefore I did not chuse to go to Chatham with him, but was rather willing to take my chance at Portsmouth.

It was not long before the *Royal Sovereign* was ordered into harbour to be paid off, but the *St. George* was the first ship, and ours the next. The boatswain told me to make myself easy, for I should stay with him till the *Sandwich* came in, and if she went to Plymouth, he would send me down in her. In a little time after, the ship was paid off; and it was not long before I went on shore, which I was very glad of; and my joy was so great on this occasion, that I ran up and down, scarcely knowing how to contain myself.

I had now been on board the *Royal Sovereign* one year, and almost nine months, without being on shore all the time; nor was I in the least suspected of being a woman. On December 21st, 1762, I went to the boatswain's house, and eat and drank there; this being much about Christmas time, the weather was very cold. As I was going down the town, I met the coxswain of the cutter to the *Sandwich*, which very much surprised me. I immediately asked him whether he belonged at that time to the *Sandwich?* Why yes, I do; and your master ordered me to tell you to come on board to see him. I told him, I could not come till tomorrow. After I parted from him, I went and informed the boatswain that the *Sandwich* was arrived, and that my master had sent for me to come on board; and also mentioned to him that I would go in the morning.

Being determined to write to my father and mother that day, it being nine months since they had heard from me: accordingly I sent them a letter, the purport of which is as follows:—

Portsmouth Harbour, Dec. 25, 1762.

Hond. Father and Mother,

This comes with my kind duty to you, and hope these few lines will find you in good health, as lam at present, thanks be to God for it. I am sorry to trouble you so much with writing; but your not answering my last letter, in acquainting me how you both are, makes me very uneasy. My master is just come home; and I shall go on board to him very soon. I am lately come on shore from the *Royal Sovereign*; and long very much to see you both; but must wait with patience. Pray give my love to my brother and sister, and all friends, together with my duty and prayers for your preservation.

Your most undutiful Daughter,

Mary Lacy.

N.B. Please to direct to me as follows, For William Chandler, on board the *Royal Sovereign*, in Portsmouth Harbour.

These were the contents of the letter which I sent to my father and mother on this occasion; and, as I intimated before, that I should go on board to my master in the morning, accordingly I went down to the point, and seeing a barge I thought was the captain's, but it proved to be his clerk's, I asked the favour to let me go on board with him, which he readily complied with. This was immediately after Christmas Day. Having got safe on board, I went directly to my master's cabin, where I found both him and the gunner, who were very glad to see me. As soon as my old friend Jeremiah Paine came, who was formerly my fellow-servant, my master gave him a bottle of wine to make ourselves both merry, in telling our adventures concerning what had passed and happened to each other since our last parting.

Soon afterwards my master sent for me, and asked me whether we had drank out the wine, and eat the plum-pudding he ordered? I told him, we had. He then renewed his old story of telling the gunner that he would put me apprentice in the yard, with such other specious promises as he had often made me before. I thanked him heartily for his good will, and endeavours to serve me. Having ended this story, he began with another, which was an account of the loss he had met with since he had been at sea: but this will more properly appear in another place.

After this I went on shore to Mr. Dawkins the boatswain, and told him what my master had said to me, which he approved of, and observed, that he hoped my master would not take me up to Chatham, and there leave me, without binding me 'prentice; for, says he, "if he does, he will be very unjust to you."

I next went on board the *Royal Sovereign* to see after my box, and other things, which I brought on shore, and afterwards went to my master, who told me that my mistress was come thither in order to go to Plymouth; for his son was arrived there as carpenter of the *Bienfaisant*, and lay in sick quarters, and at the point of death; but before she could get an opportunity of seeing him he died, which was a melancholy circumstance to his father and mother, he being their only son.

When my mistress had taken an account of her deceased son's effects, she returned to Portsmouth. But the afflicted parents were so overwhelmed with grief and sorrow for the loss of their child, that their case excited compassion in every one present. Having settled their affairs here, my master and mistress went to lodge at the sign of the Ship and Castle. But I was kept constantly employed in going backwards and forwards, sometimes on board, and at others on shore to light his fire, besides doing the other common business of a lodging.

My master still continued talking to me about placing me out as an apprentice as soon as we got to Chatham; whereupon my mistress remarked, that such an action as that, could it be accomplished, would be greatly for my advantage; though by the way, she seemed very far from approving of it in general. Perceiving her inclination with respect to the matter, I thought it was a very fit opportunity for me to get clear of the apprenticeship. So when my master asked me if I would go to Chatham with him, I bluntly told him I would not; for I thought myself too old to go 'prentice.

"Well," said he, "William, I will send your money down to one Mr. John Lucas, when I get up to Chatham."

However, this promise he never performed; for, he only wrote to

Mr. Lucas concerning the money due to me whilst on board the *Royal Sovereign*, which he had no manner of business with. But the captain kept me upon the books, and paid me; which the former never did to this day.

My master and mistress being gone to Chatham, I went on board the *Royal Sovereign* again, was entered there as pursers servant, and had liberty to leave the ship when I pleased. I continued here a month, employed by men and officers, in going on shore for their necessaries: so that by frequently rowing in the boat, I became perfectly acquainted with the nature and management of it.

One day as I was going on shore with the boatswain of the *Sandwich*, he very seriously asked me if I would go 'prentice to the carpenter off the *Royal William*, whose name was Mr. M'Clean? I told him, I would let him know tomorrow; for I did not know how to deny him, being afraid they would mistrust me if I evaded it. Accordingly I went to Mr. Dawkins, the boatswain of the *Royal Sovereign*, and told him what Mr. Summers, the boatswain of the *Sandwich*, had said to me: whereupon he advised me to agree to the proposal; for that it was better to have some trade, than none at all; and added, I know him to be a good tempered man; and seven years is not for ever, so I would have you go. But the dread of being discovered that I was a woman before the expiration of my apprenticeship, was a great obstacle to this proposal.

The next day according to my promise I went on shore, and saw Mr. M'Clean waiting for Mr. Seamer to introduce me to him; for we were unacquainted with each other. In a short time after he came to me, and asked if I would go 'prentice? I told him I would. While we were thus talking, Mr. M'Clean came up to me, and asked if I would he his apprentice? I answered, "Yes, Sir."

"Well, young man," said he, "will you go on board with me?" I told him I would, provided he would let me have a boat to go on board the *Royal Sovereign*. "Young man," he returned, "you shall have a boat, and the boys shall go thither to assist you."

Accordingly I went and brought my chest, bed, and bedding, on board the *Royal William*.

My master had another boy out at sea, who was not big enough to work as an apprentice in the yard, nor would the builder agree to take him; however, his own parents being dead, and his father-in-law taking no proper care of him, my master very generously maintained him.

I thought till about this time that my master was a married man;

101

for he had a woman on board with him, and a girl that was her daughter. But I soon had reason to believe they were not married, from her impudent behaviour, having had frequent opportunities of making particular observations on the conduct of loose women, and could discern their vicious inclinations immediately.

I had now been on board some time before I was bound apprentice: but the woman who co-habited with my master, began in a little time to be so familiar with me, that I thought it very extraordinary a woman who was an entire stranger to me, should become so suddenly enamoured.

Soon after this my master ordered me to clean myself, and be ready to go ashore with him, as he designed to bind me 'prentice that very day, which was the 4th of March, 1763. A boat (though it was not the proper harbour boat) being now alongside the ship to receive us, according to my master's directions, I immediately made myself ready, and prepared to go; but as this boat of ours was very old, and not capable of carrying much sail, especially when it blew a little fresh; and there being moreover a pretty brisk gale of wind, we had a great deal of trouble to reach the shore. My master then stood for the *Sandwich*, and went on board, as the boat was going on shore. We left our boat at the stern of the *Sandwich*, and went in theirs: but the wind blew so hard that we could not reach the hulk, but were forced to go to the north jett, where some caulkers stages lay alongside, at which place they had driven some nails into the piles (to climb up by) instead of ropes, which were at least sixteen feet high.

My master and the gunner had got safely up, and were walking on; but when I had almost climbed to the top, letting go the rope to take hold of the ring-bolt, my foot slipped, and I fell down into the sea; but as soon as I appeared again, the boys upon the stage soon pulled me up, though I was wet from head to foot; however, I recovered myself as well as I could.

Presently after this sad disaster my master and the gunner began to miss me; and coming back to see where I was (observing me on the stage) asked the reason why I had been so long in coming? I then told them that I had fell overboard. On which my master laughed, and sent me to a blacksmith's shop, where I immediately pulled off my coat and waistcoat to dry myself; after which he brought me out of the yard, and gave me something hot to drink, to wet the inside, for the outside was sufficiently soaked before.

My master and I went together to wait on the builder, to know if he approved of me for an apprentice; but he not being in the office, we went to his house. On asking if he was at home, the servant told us he was, and called him to us. My master then asked him, how he liked me for an apprentice?

"Why," said the builder, "I like him very well; for I think he is a stout lad."

So my master had me entered; but not as a yard servant, as he was not allowed two, being only carpenter of the *Deptford*, a fourth-rate man of war. At this time he did duty on board the *Royal William*, the carpenter of which was dead, and he had some hopes of procuring the place for himself.

I shall now proceed to relate in what manner I went to work in the yard. My master began to enquire for a quarterman for me to work under; accordingly he went to one Mr. Dunn, and found him in his cabin. After paying his compliments, he told him he had brought him a new hand, and that he hoped I should be a good boy. (And indeed I must confess he gave me a good character): and at the same time told Mr. Dunn that he hoped he would put me under a skilful workman to learn my trade; which Mr. Dunn engaged his word and honour to do: For you must know that I was a cadet, to work one week in the yard, and another on board a new ship, the *Britannia*, just launched. There being an overflowing in the harbour, all the carpenters and servants were ordered to open the men of war, to let air in, and keep the ships from rotting: But this did not last long, for we only went in the morning and evening; so that we were in the yard the greatest part of the day.

Mr. Dunn put me under one Mr. Cote to learn my business, who was a very good-tempered man, and took great pains to instruct me; he liked me very well, and seemed to be greatly delighted to hear me talk.

This affair being thus far concluded, my master went and bought me a saw, an axe and chisel, which made me very proud to think I had got some new tools to work with. On shewing them to the man I served under, he told me he would put some new shafts to them; which pleased me very well, thinking that would be very serviceable to me in beginning to learn my trade.

The first work I began upon was, to bore holes in the bottom of the ship called the *Thunderer*, which, as I was at first unacquainted with the method of doing it, proved hard work for me. This occasioned me to think I should not be able to serve out my time without being discovered.

My master and mistress living at this time on board the *Royal William*, I had no house on shore to reside in, and was therefore obliged to go on board every night; so that the boys on board our ship had a great deal of trouble to fetch me backwards and forwards: however, I soon began to lessen their trouble, by taking an opportunity to go back again in the shipwright's boat. But when it was my week to be on board, my master frequently sent me to fetch beer and other necessaries, sometimes with and sometimes without money, just as it suited his humour. However, as it happened, the ship did not lie a great way from shore, and the place where we landed was called the Hardway.

I must here observe, that the boatswain had a canoe, which I was very fond of making use of, though if I stept ever so little on one side she would overset. I continued for some time to pass and repass in her; and having learned by frequent practice the right method of rowing, could make her run with surprising expedition.

One day my master came to the yard in four-oared boat, and said he wanted me on board, bidding me get my ship ready. Accordingly I got into my canoe, and my master into his four-oared boat, when he told me he would row with me for sixpence. I replied, I would; but if I got on board first, I would insist on having the money. He promised I should. I then went alongside their boat with my canoe, that is to say over-against them; after which we started, and plied our oars as fast as we could. To enable me to proceed with greater ease and expedition, I pulled off my waistcoat, quickly overtook them, and got first on board; which when I had done, I fell a laughing at them, and called out, "Where's my money, where's my money?" He told me I should have it. But, instead of giving it me, in the evening he took all on shore and spent it among us. From this time my master every now and then challenged me to row with him; which I told him I was very willing to do whenever he was disposed for it, provided he would pay me the money when he lost. My mistress observed at the same time, that he did not do well in refusing to pay me, as he had engaged to do it.

At this time there were on board our ship a deputy purser's wife, with one Mr. Robinson and his wife, all acquaintances of my mistress, who were brought up together at Gosport. As I was then on board, they sent me for some liquor, and would often get as drunk together as David's sow: and in the height of these frolics, they would often say, "Ay, he is, ay he is, the best boy on board." In regard to Mother Robinson, I must acknowledge, she would do any kind office for me.

104

Indeed I was in general well beloved by the women, if by nobody else; and, thank God, greatly respected by my master: so that I lived a quite happy life; and went to work at the yard every day.

When we went to work on board the *Niger* frigate, I had a tool-chest made; and the quarterman, a person that I worked with, was very kind to me. I had my provisions of the king; so we made one allowance serve us, and sold the other to the purser for a guinea a quarter, as we both often dined at my master's house.

When I worked in the dockyard, I used to sell my chips at the gate; and sometimes would carry a bundle to Mr. Dawson, the boatswain, and was always welcome to his house whenever I pleased: Besides, my master frequently asked me to dine with him on Sunday, if they had any company on board, and then I got a sufficiency; for he would always have me wait at table. While I was laying the cloth, my mistress would stroke me down the face, and say, I was a clever fellow. Which expression made me blush.

Frequently after supper my master would ask me to favour them with a song, adding, that if I condescended to this, it would oblige them very much. Wherefore to divert them, I commonly sung them two or three songs, which often made them merry, till about twelve o'clock; when my master would order me with three more boys to row them to the Hard at Portsmouth Common; after which they made us a present to buy a little beer; but we made all the haste back we could.

I continued working in the dock; and my master and mistress were very fond of my company, because I could sing to please them. When I came home in the evening, I generally sat down by them, and sung a merry song, with which they were greatly delighted; so that I thought it no manner of trouble to serve them either by day or night. And thus having the good will of all, I lived very happy.

One evening my master had some company came on board to see him, and I was appointed to wait at table. When my mistress kept calling so repeatedly, I concluded my master was not married to her: This suspicion occasioned me to observe to my fellow-servant, (whose name was Jonathan Lyons) that I thought they were not man and wife; at which he fell a laughing: however, I did not care speak much about it, lest I should not say right. So it passed on for some time.

A little while afterwards, coming on board in the evening, my master and mistress had some words; and the woman that was acquainted with my mistress, let me into the secret of their intimacy. "You must know," said she, "your mistress, as you call her, was never married to your master, nor ever will, for she is at present married to another; her lawful husband lives at this time at Greenwich Hospital, and his name is Mr. ———."

To proceed with the rest of my adventures. My master having no other ship, we lived on board; though he often talked of taking a house on shore, which (by the way) my fellow servants and myself heartily wished he would do. But he now began to take more and more notice of me every day; yet he was very kind to us; and would not allow me to clean his shoes, nor the knives and forks, or do anything when I came home from the dockyard, except when there were company on board, and then I waited at table.

It appeared my master formed a strong suspicion that I had got a sweetheart who lived upon the Common, and was often talking about it, advising me to be cautious, and not to marry till I was out of my time; and then he would give me a wedding dinner. Indeed I often laughed to myself, when I considered that my master imagined I went a courting; for I was acquainted with several young women, which occasioned him to think that I was rather too familiar with them: and truly very glad I was he thought so; for in that case he could have no mistrust of my sex.

One day when I was on board, and my master shore, my mistress and Mr. Robinson were disposed to make themselves merry: accordingly they sent me to shore to fetch some liquor, which they repeated so often that I was quite tired; and kept it up till they had spent all their money, but did not know where to get more: and I remember, that I once mentioned in their hearing, my going to one Mr. Penny to bring liquor for my master on credit. This opportunity they thought was a specious pretext to get more liquor. My mistress therefore sent me for a pint of rum, and desired me to tell them, my master would pay for it when he came on shore. Accordingly I went and brought the rum; imagining, that as my master allowed me to call her mistress, he would not blame me for fetching it, having given me no orders to the contrary. So that, according to the proverb, with this liquor they got as drunk as pipers.

On my master's coming on board in the evening, he soon perceived what they had been at; but took no notice, only sat and laughed at them, he being very well acquainted with their frolics. But they were so pleased with me for bringing this liquor, that my fellow servants seemed almost to envy me; and said, they believed my mistress and I were too intimate, and that they wished she was so fond of them; for they observed, she was always giving me something or other, and that it was enough to spoil the most sober man in the world, because she would never go on shore but I must go with her, and then went in all sorts of company, both good and bad. But, thank God, it happened very well for me, as I never went to these licentious places but it occasioned me to be very much on my guard, and to be extremely cautious what sort of company I kept.

I must here reflect with gratitude, that if some sort of people had been witness to the variety of scenes of life that have passed under my observation, the fight would have made their very hair stand on end: Some were quarrelling and fighting; others had their eyes knocked out, and afterwards kicked out of doors; and sometimes even driven from their warm beds, and had no person of reputation or humanity to receive them. Therefore all these disagreeable prospects should teach us to amend in ourselves what we see amiss in others. These considerations occasioned me often to think with great sorrow, that I had done mischief enough in leaving my parents, without their knowledge or consent; and hope this will be an example to all others not to be guilty of the like imprudence.

I shall now proceed (according to my journal) to relate what passed concerning the pint of rum I brought to my mistress; for my master had been on shore to pay the beer, but not the rum: Mr. Penny, it appears, had then given him to understand, that there was a pint of rum to pay. "A pint of rum," said my master "I have had none. Do you know who came for it?"

"Yes," replied Mr. Penny, "I know the boy when I see him."

Upon that my master came on board, and asked if we had fetched any rum on board for anybody from Mr. Penny's? They all answered, No. He then said, "I shall find it out; therefore you had better let me know before I go on shore." Hearing this, I went and told my mistress what had passed on the occasion; but she would not suffer me to tell him till we went on shore.

My master soon after ordered us all to go on shore along with him: He going first into the house where we had the beer and rum, found there the carpenter of the *Thunderer*, who was present when I fetched the rum; but he would say nothing to my master, lest he should affront my mistress, because she was a very good customer. Upon this we were called in, when my master asked Mr. Penny which of us all it was that brought the rum? Mr. Penny began at top, and narrowly examining the physiognomy and habit of everyone till he came to me, then said, "This is the boy who fetched it."

My master then said, "William, did you fetch it?"

"Yes, Sir," returned I; "but I shall be glad to speak with you."

Hereupon we both went out.

"Well," said he, "did your mistress send you for any rum?"

I told him, "Yes."

"Why," says he, "did you not tell me before you came on shore?"

"Because," I replied, "my mistress would not let me; though I was sure you would soon find it out."

"Well," says my master, "go in and get some beer."

Accordingly we went in, and got two or three pots of beer, and then went on board again.

After this my mistress came to me, and asked if my master had found it out? "Found it out!" Said I, "yes, to be sure he has; and you had better have let me told him before I went on shore, and then no one would have known anything of the matter; but now everybody knows it."

Soon after my master came on board, but took no notice of the above-mentioned affair.

He began now to think of taking a house on the Hardway, for he heard there was one to let, which we were glad of. I still went to the yard to work; but was forced to go round to Gosport, which was two full miles walk twice every day. And after I got home in the evening, was forced to hail the ship; and when the wind was in the east they could not hear me; therefore I was often obliged to stand in the wind and cold till I was almost froze to death; which made me think how happy I should be if my master had but a house; for then I should have a good fire to sit by, and victuals to eat till the boat came for me.

I used every now and then to go on board with my canoe; and there were three apprentices that were very idle, who would take my canoe to go perrywinkling; having therefore all got into her, with a bucket to hold the perrywinkles, they set off, and got a great many, with which they returned, and came alongside the ship; but beginning to play their pranks, they overset her, lost all the perrywinkles, and narrowly escaped being drowned, though two of them could swim, who getting at last alongside the ship, with our assistance got on board. It was with much difficulty we saved poor Abraham Mills, who was very near drowned; and my canoe left bottom upwards.

These boys were continually plaguing me to go with them; but

I was always afraid, lest they should overset her, for the least thing would do it: so that I never had the courage to venture with them; and whenever they got in first to go on shore, I would go in the harbour boat; and on our return, would get in my canoe and go on board.

It came now to my turn to keep watch at night, when my master ordered me to watch four hours, and then call somebody else. Mine being the middle watch, I was ordered to strike the bell every half an hour. Accordingly I went forwards, and struck as I was directed. However, being but a cadet in the yard, my master ordered me to go a fishing with him in Stock Bay, when he caused me to sit down all the way backwards and forwards to sing. One day it being very wet, the fish began to bite very fast, and my master would not leave off till the tide obliged him to retire. We the weighed, set our sails, got safe into the harbour, and safe on board, though in a very wet condition.

Sunday following, my master had given an invitation to an old landlord and his family (where he once lodged) to come and take a dinner with him on board; therefore he ordered me and my fellow servant to go and fetch them from the shore. I immediately cleaned myself, put on my blue jacket, went for them, and rowed them to the ship; and while they were at dinner, I waited at table. My mistress asked them how they liked me?

"Why I think," said they, "that he is a very handy lad."

To which my mistress answered, "Ay, and he is a sweet tempered lad too:" for she was then in good humour; and made me eat and drink of all that was prepared for the guests.

When the evening was come, we prepared to row the visitors on shore again; and as the wind began to blow pretty fresh, I haled the boat alongside the ship, put the mast and sails up, and set sail. We had a fair wind to the shore, and landed them at the place where we took them from in the morning: we afterwards tried to work out from the shore, and tack about backwards and forwards, but could make no way, which obliged us to lower the sails, and pull the boat out to the stern of the *Essex*, and then hoist sail again; but the wind being north-west, was right against us, and blew so hard that we could not carry sail enough to work on the other shore. However, we ventured to sail; but when we got over against the hulk, there came a squall of wind, which almost overset us.

I had got the main sheet in one hand, and the tiller in the other; but I let them go, and luffed her up, as she was almost full of water, be-ing very old, and not having ballast enough to carry much sail. In this distress I struck sail, and let her drive where she would. We then drove down Palchester Lake, where fortunately for us a lighter lay moored, on board of which was a man, who seeing us coming, hove out a rope, which I caught hold of, took a turn with it, and moored her to the lighter. We then went on board, and staid all night; for we were as wet as we possibly could be, not having so much as a dry thread about us. As there was no fire, we were forced to sit up all night in our cloaths; and thanks be to God we were so well off, seeing it was a great mercy we were not drowned.

My master rose in the morning, and looked about the harbour to try if he could see or hear anything of us. Getting no intelligence of us, he began to be frightened, and at length concluded we were drowned. But I had ample reason to be thankful to Divine Providence, which had preserved me in all my extremity and trouble, and continued to help me; for we bailed the water out of the boat, and then rowed up to the ship. Before we came on board, we saw our master looking out of the stern gallery; who perceiving us coming, made up a large fire for us as soon as we came on board, and gave me a pair of dry stockings to put on.

Having got some dry cloaths, my master and I went to the dock-yard, but too late for my call: whereupon I went to the clerk, who taking my checque off, I went to work till night. When I came on board in the evening, I was very glad to sit down by the fire; but did not sit there long before I turned into my hammock; for being greatly fatigued, I found I wanted rest most, and could sleep without rocking, having been up all night before.

It unfortunately happened that I could not continue to work in the yard, as I wanted to do, being obliged to go to work with my master every other week on board the ships, which in a great measure hindered me from learning my trade. I therefore asked my master to let me go into the yard to work. He told me the yard was so far off, that it was not worth my while to go down to work. I observed to him, that as I met with so many interruptions, I should never be able to learn my trade. Well, said he, if you don't learn to build, you will learn to pull pieces: for it seems my master expected to be the car-penter of the *Royal William*, having done duty on board her for some time: in that case he was to have two boys allowed him in the yard; this, however, never happened; one Mr. Williams being appointed for her. I afterwards learned he was to have a third rate, which has as many boys as a second-rate, though there is ten shillings difference.

My master had now obtained a warrant for a new ship that was building at Lippe, called the *Europa*; and, coming home one night, I happened to be on shore, when he said to me, "Well, master Chandler, what news now?"

"Sir," I replied, "I don't hear of any."

"Why," said he, "have not you heard that you and I are to go to plough, and that I am to hold the plough, and you drive the horses?"

I found he was only joking; because he had got a new ship building in the country at Lippe.

Next time I had occasion to go to the dock, wanting to come on board sooner than usual, I went in my canoe, and got alongside the shore; but the wind blowing pretty fresh, I could not keep her off the shore, nor get a head. Mr. Dawkins of the *Royal Sovereign* seeing me in distress, sent his four-oared boat to fetch me on board, otherwise I should certainly have been drowned. As I came by the ship, he said to me, "Your canoe will be your coffin one day or other;" and kindly added, "if your boys are so lazy, that they will not carry you down to the dock in their duty-weeks, I will send my boy to fetch you." I returned him thanks for his kindness.

I shall next proceed to relate what passed concerning the young woman who lived at Mr. Dawkins's house, which place I often went to. Being there one evening, he asked me to stay till morning, as he himself was to remain on board all night; and moreover, the maid insisted on my promising to stay there. Having consented, we sat at cards till twelve o'clock; when some young women, who spent the evening with us, went home. I then asked the maid where I was to lie? She answered, there was no place but with her, or her mistress. I told her I would lie in her bed. Accordingly she lighted me up to her chamber. Perceiving her forwardness, I thought it was no wonder the young men took such liberties with the other sex, when they gave them such encouragement; and I am compelled, for the sake of truth, to say this much of the women; but am far from condemning all for the faults of one or two: however, when a young woman allows too much freedom, it induces the men to think they are all alike.

I must confess, that if I had been a young man, I could not have withstood the temptations which this young person laid in my way: for she was so fond of me, that I was ever at her tongue's end; which was the reason her master and mistress watched her so narrowly. In short, there was nothing I could ask that she would refuse; and, to make me the sensible of it, my shorts were washed and prepared for me in the very best manner she was able.

One day my master took me to task about keeping this young woman company; adding, that he was afraid she would be a means of corrupting my morals, since her brothers were given to dancing, and night-revelling. But when she asked me to go amongst them, I gave a flat denial on that head. She then enquired the reason why I would not go? I answered, That it generally brought young people into bad habits and company of loose behaviour, destroyed their constitution, and rendered them incapable (by being up all night) to do their business the following day. Finding me determined not to comply with her solicitation, she never after that time asked me to go with them.

I was now a yard servant; and lived at my master's house on shore, who told me that I should have a new suit of cloaths, and not go so shabby as I was. To this end he went to Mr. D—ge, a taylor in Gosport, and ordered him to come on Sunday morning to take measure of me for a new suit of cloaths. The taylor came as he was directed; and my master gave me my choice of the colour, for which I thanked him, and fixed upon a blue, which he seemed well pleased with: and I was not a little proud to think that I should have good and decent apparel to appear in, as I could then walk out on Sundays with the young women.

When I had got my new cloaths, one Edward Turner, who messed with me when I was on board, and between whom and myself there had always subsisted a very intimate friendship, came on shore, and invited me to walk out with him. Having first asked leave of my master, which he readily granted, we accordingly set out; and when in each others company, we were always talking about the young women, or of working in the yard; for Wednesday and Saturday being the women chip days, I soon made myself acquainted with some of them; and found them at all opportunities as well pleased in procuring the acquaintance of the men as in any place in England.

One day the above-mentioned Edward Turner invited two young women to come and take a dinner with him and his messmate on board the *Royal William*; for on my coming to live on shore, he got another messmate to dine with him. On this occasion, my trusty friend Edward, asked me if I would come and dine with him at the same time and place? And then, says he, I will help you to a sweetheart. I told him, if my master would permit me to come, I certainly would. He accordingly gave me leave; and I immediately went down to Gosport on board the *Royal William*, that was brought into dock to have a thorough repair. But the young women not being come, I was very impatient till they arrived, for I wanted much to see them.

We had a leg of mutton and turnips, and a fine plum pudding provided, with plenty of gin and strong beer, which I considered as a grand entertainment for me and the young ladies. I had not been long on board before they came; on the sight of whom, I went immediately and paid my compliments to them; and we soon became acquainted together, they not forgetting to ask where I lived, which I as readily told them. We were very merry with our new acquaintance; and I soon found that Vobbleton Street was the place of their residence. This street in Portsmouth Town is inhabited with divers classes of people; so that I soon found what sort of company I was with.

Having spent the day on board with a good deal of mirth and humour, we agreed to escort the young women home: and indeed it was very proper we should.

Having therefore trudged to town with them, we were prevailed upon by their importunities, to stay supper with them: so that with one thing or other, we tarried there so late, that we could not get a boat to carry us over the water; at which I began to fret, lest my master should severely reprimand me. For as I had my new cloaths on, and knew that I must go to the yard to work in the morning, it really made me very uneasy. However, to remove this difficulty, the young women insisted on our lying together at their house.

I knew not what to do in this case: but recollecting that this young man had no suspicion of my being a woman, we went to bed together; and lay till four o'clock in the morning, when we got up and went to dock. As we were walking along, he asked me what I thought of those girls, and how I liked them? I told him, I thought they were a couple of merry girls.

As soon as I came up to the place of call, the people began to stare at me, which brought scarlet in my face; and asked me where I had been all night? I made them no answer; only went to the clerk, to desire leave to go home and pull off my cloaths, and put others on to work with; which he readily granted.

After this, lest I should meet my master, I crossed the water: but I was no sooner got home than I found that he was gone round to look for me, thinking he would meet me coming round that way. I went upstairs, pulled off my cloaths, and put others on; and desired my master's nephew to take no notice to his uncle that I was come home; which he promised not to do. But my mistress neither hearing or seeing anything of me, and being more inquisitive than usual, as soon as she got up in the morning, went upstairs, and looked in my chest; on seeing my cloaths there, she came down, and severely reproved the boy for not telling her of it.

In the evening when work was over, my fellow servant and I went home; and the first word my master said to me was, "How do you do, master Chandler? I hope you and she lay very close together last night?"

"No, Sir, I did not lie with any woman last night; for I lay with Edward Turner."

"I have only your bare word for that," said he.

"Sir," I replied, "you may believe me if you please."

My master, it is true, believed I was very fond of some young woman or other; and so I was; but not in that manner he thought I was guilty of. However, he was not angry with me for lying out all night; and I took pretty good care not to stay out again. As for my fellow servant, he was always asleep as soon as he came home from dock; and though we lay together six months, I was in no danger of his finding me out, as he was no sooner abed but asleep.

It now happened that my master's young nephew lay along with us; and I was more afraid of him than of the other, because he was not so sleepy; though I considered, that being so young, there could be no apprehension of danger from him.

My master asked me sometimes on a Sunday, whether I would go along with him, or meet my sweetheart? I often chose rather to accompany my master to Blocks fort, where we often staid some time; and I might eat or drink any thing I pleased; for he was a very good-natured man to me: notwithstanding which, there was one thing in him that I disliked, which was, that he would swear very much. This unjustifiable practice I was very averse to; and could not help thinking he was quite blameable in living with a woman as a wife, that was every day contributing to ruin him; for I often heard it reported, that he might have married with a woman of fortune, who in all likelihood would have made him a very happy man.

The pernicious effects of his criminal cohabitation with this person appeared in several instances, and particularly in the following one: In a short time after we came to live on shore, she used to fetch so much liquor in his name that he could scarcely discharge the debts she had contracted, which very frequently soured his temper, and occasioned him with some heat to tell her he would turn her out of doors; which made me think I should soon have new mistress.

Some time after this, my master had some business at Blocks Fort, and she determined to follow him, but with no other intention than to scandalize him in the worst manner she could, which produced a great many reproachful words betwixt them.

When my fellow-servant and I came home from work at night, we found the doors fast, which occasioned us to go to the next house to enquire if the key was there. The people told us my mistress had left it. Having got the key, we both went in, supped, and retired to bed; but had not been there long before our mistress came, and brought a waterman along with her; for she had been at Gosport amongst her old acquaintances. She soon called for me. I told her I was coming down; which I did without the knowledge of my bedfellow, who never heard me either get out of bed or in again; so that I could never have had a more agreeable bedfellow in my life: for if I has lain a-bed a week, and ever so earnestly wished for such a one, I could scarce have such another.

When I came down, I found the waterman along with my mistress, who began haleing and pulling me about in such a manner, that I could not tell what was the matter with her, or the reason for her doing so. Afterwards I found that she wanted some beer; for she said she was thirsty. Accordingly I went and brought a pot of ringwood: and it being summer time, she sat at the door to drink it; over against which there being a wheelbarrow, I went and sat down upon it. My mistress observing me, came and placed herself in my lap, stroking me down the face, telling the waterman what she would do for me: so that the few people present could not forbear laughing to see her sit in such a young boy's lap as she thought I was. However, she had not been long in this situation before my master came home, and passed by her as she sat there; but taking no notice that he saw us, went in doors. And indeed I was very much frightened lest he should beat me; but I thought he could not justify be angry with me, as it was all her own fault.

I went then to try the door, to discover if my master had locked it, which he had done; therefore I told her the door was locked, and that we must both lie in the street. Upon which, she said, she would go to Gosport, and that I should go along with her.

As we were thus talking together under the window, my master overhearing her say, she would set off for Gosport, was resolved to give us something, if it was only a good wetting, to remember him before we went; and accordingly in a moment he threw up the window, and soused us all over with a chamber-pot full of water; which made me fall into such a fit of laughter, that my sides were ready to burst. In short, I could not refrain from laughing, to see what a pickle she was in.

After this a thought came into my head that I would again try whether the door was locked before we set off for Gosport, and, as I wished, found it open. I did not stop to tell her of it, but immediately took off my shoes and stockings, ran upstairs, pulled my bedfellow out of his place, and got into it myself; for I supposed if my master came up to thresh me, he would lay hold of him first, and then I should have time to get away. However, as good luck would have it, he did not concern himself with me; but vented his anger on my mistress when she came in, telling her she might go to the waterman again, and would not let her come to bed.

In the morning my bedfellow John Lyons wondered how he came into my place; for he had heard nothing about the matter, being such a sound sleeper. We both went as usual to work at the dock. But when we came home I was under most terrible apprehensions that my master would chastise me; but to my great comfort, he did not seem to take the least notice of what had passed on the occasion. Having now given you some account of the behaviour and disposition of my mistress, I shall leave her for a while, and proceed to other occurrences.

My master found out at length that I had a sweetheart, who lived at Portsmouth Common, but in what part he could not tell, though he imagined he should find it out some time or other; but after all, he was mistaken in the person; for he thought of a young woman that lived in Hanover Row, which was the very house I went to; and therefore resolved one day or other to go at dinner time to enquire for me, imagining that to be the best time to find me there. Accordingly my master took an opportunity to go to the place where he believed I frequently resorted to; but when he went there, the people happened to be out.

When I came home at night from the dock, the first word he said to me was, "Your servant, Mr. Chandler, pray how does your wife do, that is to be? For I have been at the house today, but the people were not at home; however, I suppose you know where they are gone to."

At first I could not tell what he meant by it, not knowing that he had been at the house, or who had told him that I went there. I made answer, "A wife, Sir! that is more than I think of yet."

He then said, "You can't make me believe so."

"Sir," said I, "I don't know who you are talking about."

"No!" replied he, "don't you know the house that has steps to go up at the door?"

"Steps to the door!" said I, "I don't know what you mean."

Immediately upon that I recollected the house in Hanover Yard upon the Common; and asked him (describing such a house) if it was that he meant?

"Oh!" said he, with a little raillery, "you have thought of it at last."

Which in fact was so far true: but I did not care who knew that I went there; for the woman was most certainly a very good friend to me, though she knew not what I was.

At last, my master said to me, "Well, William I would have you stay till you are out of your time before you marry; and if she be a sober girl, I'll give you a wedding dinner."

Indeed I could not help laughing at what he had said to me about going a courting; and I was very glad to find he thought so.

I now began frequently to talk to the young women, and soon became a tolerable proficient in the art of courtship, but was very cautious of what I said to them; for our sex are so weak as to think that if a young man does but once speak to them, he must become a sweetheart at once. In this respect we are greatly deceived; but they who know as much of both sexes as I do, would be of a different opinion; therefore would not have you trust too far, lest you should be disappointed. But true it is, my master would ever be pestering me with something or other about the young women; and my mistress was so evil inclined, that she thought everybody as bad as herself.

One night when I came home from work from the dock, I found myself pretty much indisposed, and seeming somewhat uneasy, I sat down to rest myself, which my mistress took the opportunity of making a ground of invective; for thinking I was fast asleep, she began to question my fellow-servant about the cause of my indisposition. He said, he knew nothing farther than that he heard me say, I was not well.

"Ay," said she, "I am sure he is ill indeed, for he has no life in him; he never used to sit down sleeping in this manner before;" little thinking I heard every word she uttered. When I began to move, she thus addressed me: "Well, Bill, what is the matter?" I told her, nothing more ailed me than being a little sick, and out of order.

She said, "I am sorry for it;" and declined making any more mention of her suspicions at this time: and for my part I took no farther notice of what passed. She, nevertheless, told my master a strange pack of stuff; but he had too much good sense to take notice of it.

When we sat down to supper, he would often say to me, "Well, master Chandler, how do you find yourself now? I hope you are something better."

Nor would my mistress be behindhand in her questions and insinuations; and frequently gave me very great liberty to be free with her, even more than I could wish to subscribe to, or acknowledge; but I took it from whence it came.

Thus much is certain, that she did not know what to think of me; but verily believed I kept company with the above-mentioned young woman in Hanover Row on the Common, though she was greatly deceived; for I seldom went out with any young woman except Elizabeth Cook, who being very fond of my company, would not leave me, which gave me some cause to believe the intimacy would bring trouble on me one day or other. I thought therefore, the best way to put an end to this matter, would be, to frame some cause of dislike in her conduct: to effect which, a very favourable opportunity soon offered; for going on board the *Royal Sovereign* to see her, where her master and mistress then were, I observed a man to be very familiar with her: and in truth, her master himself, who was frequently giving me the most wholesome instructions, seemed very glad of the occasion to mention to me a hint of their too great familiarity.

One evening I went to the house of the young woman's father, and asked for Miss Betsy. Her mother answered, she was gone out; but she expected her home very soon. I therefore waited till her return, when we took a walk together.

After a little conversation, by way of prelude to my design, I told her, I thought it would be best for us to break off acquaintance; because it plainly appeared to me, I was not the only person she gave her company to, mentioning at the same time what I saw on board the *Royal Sovereign*. On this, she seemed greatly confused; and asked what I could mean by questioning her constancy; adding, that she never once entertained so much as a single thought about any person besides myself, and that if I would promise her marriage she would not grudge to stay twelve years for me. To which I made no other reply than that from what I had already seen, I ran the risque of buying a bad bargain, and then I should be in an unhappy situation indeed. Notwithstanding all this, she was determined not to quarrel with me on any pretence: so that not knowing what to do with her, it passed off for that time; and we still continued our walks as opportunity served.

Soon after this, some misunderstanding happened betwixt her parents and herself; the consequence of which was, she took a room by the Common, to follow the business of a *mantua*-maker, to which she has served an apprenticeship, and could get a good livelihood by it. She gave me an invitation thither to see her as often as I pleased, which happened but seldom, on account of my great distance from it; though this was sufficient to keep our courtship alive.

But my watchful guardian, Mr. Dawkins, for so I may call him, discovered that we continued our intimacy; at which he seemed much displeased; and was astonished that I could not penetrate into her real character, nor see my own folly (as he thought) in persevering in such an inconsiderate proceeding; for it must be confessed, he wished me as well as if I had been a child of his own: so that he could not forbear speaking, when he plainly saw (as he imagined) the trouble I was bringing on myself. But I knew myself to be clear of these things; nevertheless, ought to return Mr. Dawkins thanks for his care over me, since he always supposed me to be a man.

I shall now return to my master and mistress. This pretended or nominal wife had greatly run him in debt for liquor. At a certain time, my master had occasion to go to Gosport; and she resolved to follow him thither. When they both got there, they began to quarrel, and had high words with one another: whereupon he left her, and came home.

As soon as he returned to his house, he shut the front windows, fastened the doors, took the little boy into the room, and caused him to pull off his cloaths, which induced the poor boy to think he was going to flog him: he then ordered the boy to put his two thumbs upon the table, which when he had done, my master put his two thumbs upon the boy's, and compelled him to declare truly, who had been to see his aunt, and what liquor she had had; for, said he, "if you don't tell me truth, I will flog you as long as I am able"

The poor boy dreading the worst, confessed there had been a gentleman to see his aunt, who had a bowl of punch; that she had some beer and brandy for herself; and that whenever any person came to see her, she would send him off for such sorts of liquor as best suited their palate. On which confession he was very well pleased; and directed the boy, with some visible marks of satisfaction, to put on his cloaths.

My master had no sooner opened the door and windows than his wife came in; but he took no notice of anything at that time. A day or two afterwards, he went to pay Mr. Lambeth for the liquor; then went home and called her to account, enquiring what she had done with so much liquor.

A short time after this, a more disagreeable circumstance than the above happened, which put us all to a stand, and is as follows: My master having occasion to go upon some business to Gosport market, was arrested, carried to a spunging-house, and confined there the whole night. As soon as I was acquainted with the affair, I was determined (in company of my fellow-servant) to go and see him. When we found the house, I enquired if Mr. M'Clean was there? and was answered, "Yes." After telling them my business, and who I was, the officer's servant took us upstairs, where we found him in a lockup room. But on seeing him in such a place, I could not forbear crying. Whereupon he asked what I cried for? Telling him my reasons, he bid us make ourselves easy, for that he believed tomorrow he should be out; and then caused us both to sit down and refresh ourselves.

After this we returned home, went to bed, and in the morning got up to our work; when we found by the discourse of one of our company, that he had seen my master going to Winchester jail that morning in a post-chaise.

Next morning I set off for Winchester; but did not know one step of the road beyond Farnham; at which place, I was obliged to enquire what road to take. And indeed I thought I never should get there, the passengers being so few to that place; and so much up and down hill, that I could not see Winchester till I came almost into it. It is fifty miles there and back, which I walked in one day.

I soon found out the jail; and having made my errand known, with the reasons for my coming, and a multiplicity of other questions that were asked me, at length the turnkey let me in. But when I saw the felons with their chains on, it much grieved me, to think that my master must stay in such a place. However, I followed the turnkey, who led me from one room to another, till at last he brought me to my master; but could scarce believe his own eyes: nor could I refrain from crying the very instant I saw him; who to moderate my grief, he assured me he should be out again in a little time. "But why," says he, "do you keep crying?"

"Sir," returned I, "to see you in such a place as this."

He replied, "There are a great many more in this place."

"Yes, Sir; but you are not like them."

"Why not like them?" Said he.

"Because, Sir, they are put in for robbing, but you are not."

When I came home, I found my fellow-servant and the little boy together. After I had related to them what I thought proper, we went to bed; and in the morning went to work as usual. However, very fortunately for my fellow-servant and myself, there was one Mr. Colman in the dockyard, who kept a cabin for the shipwrights. He being very lame, always carried his chips home in his boat; and if his boys did not come down to carry them, which sometimes they neglected to do, he used to prevail on me to carry them to his house, and would often make me stay supper; and sometimes ordered my fellow-servant to go along with me, where we were sure of being well satisfied, and sent home contentedly; for Mr. Lambert at this time had refused to let us have any farther credit, which in truth put us often into great freights.

At length my mistress came home, and immediately began stripping the house; and carrying the furniture to the pawnbroker's; which indeed was the only method that could be taken to procure us some victuals: and I am sure we had little enough from her; but our neighbours kindness supplied the deficiency. My master was so much in debt that we could not expect any money from him; therefore we were obliged to shift, and live as well as we could. My mistress seldom lay at home above a night in the week, and went abroad in the morning: so that for the remaining part of the week, when I came home from work at night, was obliged to go from house to house as it were in my master's name, or rather on his account, which was upon the whole a very fatiguing situation to me.

It happened once when my mistress was not at home, that I lay in her bed; and Mr. Colman, who was obliged to pass by our door to the waterside, always gave me a call, upon which I jumped out of bed, and told him from the window that I was coming; which occasioned him to spread a report all over the yard, that I was abed with my mistress, because I had looked out of her window; and this they believed was true, (though they did not blame me for it) and the more so because she would frequently come into the yard, and take me with her over to Gosport into those lewd houses in South Street, where I was obliged to be very free with the girls, and where I was promised first to have the daughter of one, and then of another for my wife; so that I had plenty of sweethearts in a little time; and got myself a fine name among them. As I was frequently walking out with some of them, the men of the yard concluded that I was a very amorous spark when in the company of women.

My master still continued in jail; and I did not know when he would be able to get out. It happened however, that the *Africa* was ordered to sea, the carpenter of which keeping a pawnbroker's shop at Gosport, did not care to go with her; and well knowing what unhappy circumstances my master was in, and that both their ships were of the same rate, thought he would be glad to go in his room, rather than lie in a jail: he therefore wrote a letter, which I was appointed to carry. This office I undertook very readily.

When my master had read the letter, he objected to the proposal in it; as he chiefly wanted all his creditors to agree to a composition, in order for his enlargement. But this the plaintiff refused to consent to, insisting on the whole of the debt being paid, which it was not in his power to do; and he could have willingly turned me over to him as a satisfaction for the debt. But the creditor wanted somebody to pay the money down at once, or to receive all my wages till the whole was paid. My master, however, would not consent to this, unless he would take me altogether, and receive my money from one pay-day to another, as he could think of no other way of discharging the debt. But this Mr.—— not agreeing to, I set out for home again.

Soon after this, my mistress, as I used to call her, came to me in the yard, and desired that I would come to her at the sign of the Coach and Horses. Accordingly at night, when I left off work, I went and enquired for her at the place where she had directed me; and after meeting with her there, she asked me if I would go to the play with her, and a young woman called Sarah How, who indeed was a very handsome girl.

"If you will go with us," said she, "I will give you a ticket"

I promised to her I would go; and from that time the above Sarah How became very free and intimate with me; nor did I ever go to town without calling to see her, when we walked out together; and my mistress believed she had helped me to very agreeable company.

However, the night I went to the play, my mistress took care to be there; and when I came back I was to lie at Mrs. Cook's; but how, and in what manner, I did not yet know. On asking them therefore, where I was to lie ? they answered, that I must lie along with them; for they had but one bed, and there were no less than four to lie in it; but it happened to be a very large one. They made me get into the bed first, which I did with my breeches on: but indeed I never had such an un-easy night's lodging before in my life; for they pinched me black and blue; and glad was I at the appearance of morning, when I got up and went to work. But if anybody had assured me there were such women existing, I could not have believed it: but God forbid there should be many such!

About this time Mr. Simmons sent for me to come to him directly; and purport of the whole message was, that he had agreed to pay the jail fees to set my master at liberty. My mistress being returned, and present at the time, when she saw Mrs. Simmons give me half a guinea to hire a horse and set off, took it out of my hand, and went to the Dolphin in North-street, Gosport, and there procured a horse to carry us both, though it was not intended she should go, yet being determined upon it, the horse was got ready, and away we set off Jehu-Dobbin-like.

I drove on pretty fast all the way, which occasioned my mistress's cloaths to become quite loose about her; and going through Waltham, the people took me to be a sailor, and that I had got my Moll (as they term them) with me; for her cloaths were almost off.

At last we reached Winchester, about nine o'clock at night; but too late to be admitted into the jail. Next morning being Sunday, my master could get no business done; I was therefore obliged to return back; and in the afternoon about seven o'clock, set off from Winchester, and rode very easy home; but had not gone far before I overtook a young woman whom I invited to ride, (well knowing what fatigue there was in walking). She at first refused my offer. I then asked her how far she had to go? She replied, "As far as Waltham." I told her she had better get up and ride. A gate being near, accordingly she got up, and we rode very gently.

She began to ask me where I came from? I replied, "From Gosport."

At which she laughed, and, said, "What! you come from Gosport!"

Whereupon I repeated to her, that I really did; and added, that if I might be so bold, should be glad to know the reason for asking me such a question? Her answer was, That she had heard great talk of Portsmouth and Gosport, and of the young men and maids there. I said, I hoped she had heard nothing bad of them. "Why," returned she, "I can't say that I have heard anything bad of them; but have often heard that the young women are too apt to be seduced."

"Supposing they are," said I, "I hope you will not condemn all for a few."

"No," says she, "I dare affirm there is a mixture of good and bad;

God forbid they should be all alike!"

In this manner we kept talking till we came to Waltham, where she alighted, thanking me for the obliging favour I had done her in giving her a lift.

I soon got safe home; and went to the dockyard to my work as usual. At length the man that arrested my master agreed to have me turned over to him; and Mr. Simmons obtained a board order from my master and him to exchange warrants. This being done, my master made over all his goods to Mr. Simmons; and after they were appraised, he went over to Winchester, paid all the jail fees, and brought my master home with him to Gosport, who soon after went on board the *Africa* at Spithead, where I went to see him; and he was, I believe, very well pleased with my visit.

Here he began to recount to me what measures he had taken to procure his enlargement; and that as he was under an absolute necessity of going to sea upon those conditions, he hoped that I would use and comply with every reasonable measure for the satisfaction of us both, till it should please God to give a more favourable turn to his affairs: and, proceeded he, "you are now to understand, that I have turned you over to Mr. Aulquier; and as soon as I am gone to sea, you must go to him for board wages, which if he does not think proper to allow, you must then board and lodge with him."

Addressing himself next to Mr. Simmons, who was then present, he said, "I hope, Sir, that if William should not like to live with Mr. Aulquier, you will be so good as to take him away, and get him board wages."

To which Mr. Simmons replied, "Yes, Mr. M'Clean, you may depend upon it I will."

Matters being thus agreed upon, Mr. Simmons and I went on shore; but I was to return on board the same evening with my master's watch, and some sea stores: however, there being some difficulty in procuring them that night, I was obliged to defer it till next day; and I lay for that time with this boy, who belonged to the same company as I did. His name was John L—l—y. He was a very sober youth; and well respected by his master and mistress.

I must now return, and proceed to relate how matters went with myself. My master was now gone to sea; and I scarce knew what steps to take; however; one Mr. Bout, cook of the *Royal William*, told me in a very friendly manner, that he would go along with me to Mr. Aulquier's house. I had never seen him but once before in my life, and that was when he kept the sign of the Bell, before he lived at Kingston, about a mile and a half from the Common, where my master had treated my mistress with a pint of wine. I thought upon the whole I liked him very well. He was, with respect to his person, a handsome man; and was bred a shipwright in Portsmouth yard.

It was now in the year 1765 when this Mr Bout went along with me to Mr. Aulquier's house. We enquired whether he was at home? To which they answered, No; but that he was expected in a short time. However, we went in; and soon after, Mr. Aulquier's wife came from the garden. I really thought she was the handsomest woman I ever saw; but her looking so much younger than he, occasioned me to think that it was impossible she could be his wife.

But to come nearer to the purpose. When Mr. Aulquier came in, I told him my master was gone to sea, and that I had no place to reside in, where I might be maintained; and that it was impossible to work without the convenient necessaries of life. He replied, I am very sensible of that; adding withal, that he did not agree to board me, because my master was to do it. To which I answered, "Sir, it is by Mr. Simmons's order I come to you."

"Well," says he, "I shall not give you any board wages; but you may come and board here."

Accordingly at night I went to his house; and had not been there long before supper was ordered, which was pork and apple pudding. When he sat down to his meal, I found I had enough to do to look at him; for he eat in such a voracious manner, that I thought he was going to disgorge it back again upon his plate. He had a brother that lived with him as a servant, to look after his horse, work in the garden, and go on errands, who supped with me when they had done, and whom I was to lay with.

In the morning I went to work in the dock as usual; and was put to the inconvenience of walking a mile backwards and forwards to and from dinner, being only allowed an hour and half for that purpose, which was very disagreeable to me.

Having thus agreed with my new master, the first thing he set me to do was to clean his shoes, knives, and forks, every night, which being a slavish and dirty employment, wore out everything I had on my back. This sort of business I had to do after my work in the yard, before I went to bed.

It may with great truth be said, that Mr. A——'s house entertained a very bad set of people: I had not been long with him before he turned me over to another man to pay his debts; and when I had worked that out, was again turned over to a third: so that being shifted from one to another, I had neither cloaths to my back, nor shoes or stockings to my feet; notwithstanding which, I was frequently (even in the dead of winter) obliged to go to the dockyard barefooted.

But my hardships did not end here; for the little provision I sometimes had, would scarce enable me to go through the work of the yard; and sometimes I had none at all. And to add to my farther miseries, as though I had not enough already, they compelled me to lay with the most vile and abandoned wretches of all denominations, who were in all respects the greatest blackguards that ever could be seen: so that for five years and a half of my apprenticeship I went through as great a variety of hardships as any person in my station could possibly experience.

One evening after my work at the dockyard, though in very rainy weather, I was sent with the cart to the Common to fetch grains, which made me very wet. But as they seemed to pay very little regard to my condition, I took a candle, and went upstairs to bed; and was scarce there before I heard all the house in an uproar, the cause of which I could not immediately learn. Soon after this, I heard my master calling his wife Lewis's whore, and her mother a bitch, which caused me to make some reflection on what the young man had told me before.

At this time there was a young woman that had been a servant there three years, and knew their temper very well. This person, as soon as the noise and quarrel was over, began to think of me. She accordingly came up, and brought with her a pint of beer, and some bread and cheese, telling me not to mind their quarrels, for it was no new thing, as it very often happened. I thought within myself, they may quarrel as often as they please, for I should never quarrel with them. Next day when I came home, and the storm was over, there was nothing heard but my dear; and they appeared as loving as if no quarrel had ever happened.

Not long after this, on my coming home to dinner, I found my mistress throwing all the maids cloaths out of the chamber window, at the same time calling her all the abusive names she could think of, which set the poor maid a crying, almost ready to break her heart; all which gave me great concern; the poor woman making no other request than only desiring her wages might be paid, that she might go about her business. But when I came home at night, I found things bore a different face; for all was made up, and everything appeared quite calm: and she promised, that as soon as they removed to Gosport, she should be their chambermaid.

It being now brought to my mind, that I continued very undutiful in not having writ to my father and mother for some considerable time, I therefore took this opportunity of so doing; and shall here present the reader with the letter, which is as follows:—

Kingston, Dec. 5 1765.

Hond. Father and Mother

This comes with my duty to you both, hoping these few lines will find you in good health, as I am at present, though I live but very poorly. My master, after having been in gaol some time for debt, in order to regain his liberty, was obliged to go to sea, before which he turned me over to one Mr. Aulquier. He is not so kind to me as my old master was, whose return home I will endeavour to wait for with patience, though that will not be these three years; nevertheless, I still hope I shall see him again: for he behaved towards me more like a father than a master. I hope my brother and sisters are well, and all friends that know me; and I beg you will write as soon as it suits you, to let me know how you both are. I conclude with praying for the blessing of God to attend you both, from

Your most undutiful daughter,

Mary Lacy.

These were the contents of the letter that I sent to my father and mother. I must now return to my former narrative; and inform you, that as the maid was to stay again, she and I one day began to talk about sweethearts. I told her there was a young woman I kept company with, who lived upon the Common; but that Mr. Dawkins had persuaded me to break off my acquaintance with her. I then observed, that she was a very pretty girl; and, when I lived at Kingston, she would often come to the dockyard to see me, and we sometimes walked over the Common together, and one of us afterwards accompanied the other home alternately. It happened when we had been a pretty long time in each others company, that I had scarce reached home, and taken care of the horse, before it was time to go to bed; so that I thought myself in a critical situation, because she often declared, as I have before observed, that she would stay twelve years for me, if I would promise to marry her.

Christmas Day being now come, we all went to live at Gosport, which was the more agreeable to me, as I had some time to eat my dinner; and, being made boatswain of the dock-boat, I had a shilling a week for the locking up and care of her, which was a great benefit to me, though the money was earned with great labour and fatigue; for let the weather be ever so unfavourable, I was obliged to be with her.

My master and I now agreed very well; but I did not like my new bedfellow, as he was a young man that attended the billiard table, yet of an exceeding good temper, but one that loved the women, though a little inconstant; which made me very uneasy in my mind, for fear he should find me out.

One night when I came home, there were many compliments passed betwixt us; for as I observed before, he was thoroughly good natured: so that if I wanted anything that he could get, I was sure to have it. But there was one thing I greatly disliked in him; and that was, when he came to bed, he was extremely talkative, and made a very great noise, which broke my rest. However, notwithstanding this, nobody could come into my room but I heard them; and therefore thought myself obliged to pass over this circumstance as well as I could, though the best of it was disagreeable enough.

I must take occasion to mention here, that being now pretty well settled in our house, my master bought a four-oared boat, which we put in one of the coach houses, and shoared her up; so that when I left the yard at night, I went to work upon her.

I shall now leave my master and bedfellow, and return to my old sweetheart, who still lived on the Common. On Shrove Tuesday, in the year 1766, one of her brothers came and asked me if I would go to his sister s house, as there was to be dancing there. I went accordingly the same day; but though I was ignorant of dancing, yet I thought my going might induce her to think more of me. When we came to the place, she asked me why I did not care to dance? I told her the reason (the fame which I formerly mentioned) that if I once began to revel and dance, I should not easily leave it off; that it would inevitably lead me into bad company, and render me incapable of doing my duty in the yard; all which I supposed would be sufficient to make her desist from importuning me any more on that head; and that my not going near her, would be a sure means of making her forget me.

However, I found myself mistaken; for one day, as I was going down the Common in Union Street, she happened to stand at a door; and seeing me, said, "Will, I thought you was dead."

"Why so?" returned I; "did you send anybody to kill me?"

"No," replied she; "but I thought I should never see you any more."

"What made you think so?"

"You know the reason well enough."

"Well," said I, "you are welcome to think so still, if you please; but I must be going."

"What!" said she, "you are in a great hurry now to be gone; if you was along with that Gosport girl you would not be in such haste to leave her."

I said, "I am not in such a hurry to be gone from your company, Betsy; what makes you think so?"

After this little chat, though with some seeming reserve on both sides, she asked if I would come in? I went in and sat down, and then asked her if she would come next Sunday to Gosport, and drink tea? She told me she would. Thus it was all made up again.

When Sunday came, I went down to wait the boat's coming, to help her out, which was just before my master's house, where all the servants were looking at me, and at my girl; but I paid no regard to that.

From this place we went to my old mistress, who was to make tea for us. The old gentlewoman was highly pleased to think she had met with one who was formerly her man, in company with his sweetheart, to drink tea with her. She told the young woman, I was a clever little man, and that I would make a very good husband. After tea, miss and I walked out; and then I went over the water to see her safe home.

On my coming home in the evening, all the servants asked me how my spouse did? I told them she was in good health. This occasioned Sarah to be a little jocose on me about it; however, it passed on. But, by some means or other, Mr. Dawkins had heard we kept company again; on which he was very angry with me. In order to pacify him, I went down to his house, when he immediately asked me how Miss Betsy did?

"How does Miss Betsy do!" said I; "upon my word, Sir, I don't know."

"Not know!" said he; "when you go on the Common, and call in to see her! when you are so great, and walk out together! William, I am sorry you will walk out with her, when I have told you what she is."

"Well, Sir," said I, "I am much obliged to you for your advice; but as for keeping her company, I do not; nor do I know that I shall ever speak to her again."

This matter passed over for some time; and by giving attention to my work, I thought little or nothing about things of this kind. However, one evening my fellow-servant, Sarah Chase, began talking as we were sitting together about sweethearts, and said to me in a joking manner, "I think you have lost your intended."

"Well," I replied, "I must be content."

She said, "There are more in the world to be had."

"Ay," replied I, "when one is gone, another will come."

"For my part," added she, "I have got never a one."

"Why," returned I, "I think, Sarah, you are joking with me now; are you not?"

"No," said she, "I am not;" observing at the same time, that she thought we were both in one condition.

"Well," said I, "suppose you and I were to keep company together?"

"You and I," answered she, "will consider of it."

I had not yet served quite three years of my time; nevertheless, it was agreed upon to keep company together; and that neither of us should walk out with any other person, without the mutual consent of each other. Notwithstanding this agreement, if she saw me talking to any young woman, she was immediately fired with jealousy, and could scarce command her temper. This I did sometimes to try her. However, we were very intimate together. And to give me a farther proof of her affection, she would frequently come down to the place where the boat landed, to see me, which made the people believe we should soon be married. One observed to me, "Well done, Chandler, you come on very well;" another, that she and I do it very well: and then a third would add, that I should be a cuckold before I had long been married, for that she was too large for me, and I should make but a little man; and many such like ridiculous remarks.

This young woman was always very fond of walking out with me, where we were sure of meeting with some of the shipwrights, which I well knew I should hear of the next day I went to work; when they began rallying afresh. "Ay, ay, Chandler thinks himself as fine a man as any of them, now he has got a sweetheart; let him go on, he will soon have a child sworn to him."

"Ay, ay," says another, "this is not the first he has had, for he had one on the Common; but I heard that a sailor ran away with her; however, Chandler has found a comely one in her room:" and when they saw us together remarked, "Ay, ay, there goes a woman and her husband."

Notwithstanding these things, it soon came to pass that Sarah began to have a very suspicious opinion of me, on observing I spoke to another girl; for one evening when I went in doors to ask her for some supper, she looked at me with a countenance that bespoke a mixture of jealousy and anger. It then came into my mind, that there would soon be terrible work. Whereupon I asked what was the matter with her? She told me to go to the squint-eyed girl, and enquire the matter there.

"Very well," said I, "so I can;" from hence I soon knew what was the ground of all.

It seems the tap-house woman had been telling her more of this affair at large, which brought me into a great difficulty; and indeed I lived a very disagreeable life, at home especially; since I could not get my victuals as before. On which account, I went and asked the cook what was the matter with Sarah? She said, I knew very well what ailed her.

"Well," replied I, "she will come again very soon;" during which time, when I was at home, there was nothing but grumbling. Sarah declared at the same time, that she would never speak to me again; pretending too that she did not want for a companion, which she thought would vex me, though I well knew she had none. However, to make some amends for this, the young woman sent me a letter, the contents of which are as follow:—

April, 26, 1766.

Sir,

This comes with my kind love to you, hoping these few lines will find you in good health, as I am at present; and shall take it as a favour, if, dear Mr Chandler, you will give me the pleasure of your company this evening; for you are so agreeable, that I don't know how to be without you: and if you can't come, I shall be very uneasy about you; for without you I am quite unhappy. So no more at present, from

From your sincere lover,

E. W.

When I had read this letter, I could not help laughing heartily. But I was apprehensive that the woman of the tap-house would come and tell Sarah that the letter was from this young woman; therefore I did not answer it, because I could pretend it was on account of Sarah's using me so ill; for she thought she could do with me as she pleased. Knowing therefore her attachment to me, I used to place myself at a window where I saw this young woman pass and repass in quest of me: for she could not think where I was; which induced her to watch my bedfellow, and ask him if I was not well? But he thought I was deeply in love with Sarah.

These circumstances made me seriously reflect what troubles I had brought on myself: so that by running over one thing after another, and nobody to relate my tale to, of the trouble and sorrow I had brought upon my parents, and the hardship I was like to endure myself; I say these things crowding in upon me at once, worked on my spirits at particular times to such a degree, that they robbed me of all my peace: and if at any time I endeavoured to give vent to these melancholy reflections, my expressions of grief were immediately ridiculed as the effects of love. And they would sometimes tell Sarah, that I had been crying all night for her; adding, "How can you slight him so?"

"Not I indeed," said she; "it is all his own fault; for if he had not refused me, I should not him."

And glad I was that she appeared so indifferent; for they little knew the cause of my troubles.

In this and such like manner things went on for four or five weeks, during which time I had not seen the young woman. For as I had kept myself close within doors, she had no opportunity of seeing me. She therefore determined to write me another letter, and leave it with the woman of the tap-house, which she accordingly did; and at night the woman brought it to me; of which the following is a copy for the perusal of the reader:—

Dear Sir,
This comes with my kind love to you, hoping these few lines will find you in good health; but I cannot say the same; because I am full of trouble, to think you slight my company. But I don't wonder at it; as I find you have so much love for Sarah. I know you can't love us both; and since it is your choice, I hope you will marry her, and spend your days together in pleasure. But though it is not my lot to have you, yet I hope you will be kind enough to answer this letter; or, if you will come and speak to me, I shall take it as a great favour, and that is all I can desire of you. So no more at present, from
Your sincere lover,   E.W.

When I had read the above letter, I was resolved to go and hear what she had to say. Accordingly I went: but as soon as she saw me, she fell a laughing. Upon which I told her, I should be glad to know what she wanted with me? Hereupon she said, She thought I slighted her, by keeping company with Sarah; "but now," added she, "those thoughts all vanish, for I knew your intimacy with her would not continue long."

"How came you to think so:" said I: "was it that I might keep you company?"

"Why," said she, "when I sent you the first letter, desiring to see you, you came; which was a very sufficient reason for me to think you would comply with my request."

To this I replied, "I am sensible that I came at your desire, but was wholly ignorant of your intentions, or that your inclinations tended to me; for I urged, you must consider how long I have to serve of my time."

She answered, "I don't want to be married yet, if you will only consent to keep me company."

"Pray," returned I, "what good will that do you, since you are not over hasty to be married?"

"Well," says she, "to put an end to this matter, since you seem to slight me, I will go and live in the country."

To which I answered, I did not slight her at all; and to bid her a goodnight; and home I went.

As soon as I came into the house I was set upon by Sarah; and in short, there was not any place I could go to but I was pointed at some way or other, whether at work or elsewhere; for I was looked upon as a smart fellow among the women; all which only increased Sarah's pain, by reason of my keeping this girl's company.

When I went to bed, my bedfellow said to me, "Chandler, if ever you speak to Sarah again, you deserve to have your head cut off."

On which I told him, that I should not speak to her again for some time. Indeed he was frequently speaking to me about her; and frankly told me it would be my ruin, if I did not take care of myself: "for," says he, "you look dull very often," though I knew it was not upon her account, but merely owing to my own foolishness.

It was now in the year 1767, when I came to a resolution to see my father and mother; and obtained leave for that purpose, as the navy had orders at that time to sail for the Downs the first fair wind. They sailed on the Sunday, and we got thither on Monday, when I went on shore, and afterwards passed on to Deal, where I breakfasted. After dinner I set off for Sandwich, where I had some letters to deliver; which having done, I set forward for Ash. When I came there, I went through the churchyard, and read the headstones, and saw several people I knew, though they did not recollect me. However, having a letter to deliver from a young woman to her aunt, who once knew me very well, though she had now almost forgot me, she read it; and looking at me with a mixture of surprise and joy, said, "I will be whipped if you are not Mary Lacy." This expression of hers forced a flood of tears from me; for indeed she was very glad to see me.

I had not yet seen my mother; and the above woman was extremely solicitous as well as myself to manage our interview with a suitable precaution; left from too great transport of joy, some bad consequence might happen, which very often does, in such extraordinary cases. However, it was agreed, that I should stay in another room till she had opened the matter, and prepared my mother to receive me. In a short time after, she came and told me not to be uneasy. But I could not forbear crying, being under apprehensions of my mother's fainting. She came in a little time afterwards, and ran to embrace me with all the transport and affection of a tender mother, saying, "Oh, my dear child, where have you been all this time from me, that I could not see you before?"

After mutual and affectionate salutations, we went home, where I soon found all the family very well; and took this opportunity of satisfying their earnest expectations, by recounting the various turns of fortune I had met with and gone through, during my absence for almost eight years.

Before I quit this matter, it should be observed, the young man on whose account I at first left my parents, had frequently caused enquiry to be made when I was to come home, expressing a great desire to see me: but I had no inclination to receive any visits from him. And having now been at home nine days, I signified my desire of leaving them, which caused them to shed many tears. It was now Thursday; and my time expired on the Sunday following, when, pursuant to my leave of absence, I was to be at Portsmouth.

At length, after parting from my friends, I set off, and came first to Canterbury, and soon afterwards reached Chatham by the help of a coach, where I expected to lie that night; but learning that another coach was going to London, I watched an opportunity of getting a lift in it; thinking that if I could get there at night, I should be able to reach Portsmouth in good time on Sunday. But I had not gone far behind the coach before the guide's light went out: however, he went and lighted it again; and when he returned with it, seeing me behind, he made me get down, though I told him I would pay him for it.

It now rained hard, which made me very wet; and the night being quite dark, I did not know where I was: so that in this dreary condition I had no prospect of a house to shelter myself from the inclemency of the weather. But being still inclinable to trudge on, I at length, though unexpectedly, found myself at Gravesend, where I had some refreshment. The people of the house where I had a little repast, on hearing me say that I wanted to go to London in the morning, told me I might go in one of the boats at six o'clock. I paid for my lodging and supper before I went to bed, and desired them to call me up in the morning. Accordingly I went on board; but the wind being unfavourable, we were much longer than usual in getting up to London.

Among the passengers on board this boat there was one old lady, who took me to be sea-faring man, and enquired where I came from?

I told her, "From Gosport."

"From Gosport!" said she; "who do you live with there, pray?"

I answered her, "With one Mr. Aulquier."

She replied, "I don't know him;" but asked me if I was acquainted with one Mrs. ——?

"Yes, ma'am," returned I, "I know her well; for my mistress and she are very intimate."

"Why," returned this old procuress, "she is my daughter."

At which I gave a dry look, and thought to myself she was a dextrous hand at a watch. She then asked me to take a glass of wine, and a bit of cake, which I accepted, as I knew it would do me good; and at the same time asked if I would (when they got to London) carry a little box to her daughter that lived just at hand, telling me at the same time, she would shew me London, and put me in the road to Kingston; all which I did: and when I came to the door, which her supposed daughter opened, there immediately came downstairs and addressed me as fine a girl as ever my eyes beheld, who at first sight I knew must be a kept mistress. To say the truth, this old *duenna* regaled me very handsomely; and afterwards set out for the Royal Exchange, and to see other curiosities. In this walk (which was a very extensive one) I luckily met with a carpenter of a ship, who knew me very well, and asked me where I was going? I told him to Portsmouth.

"Why," says he, "this is the wrong way; I am going down, and you may as well go with me."

Accordingly we set off: but he stopping to speak to a person, I left him, and travelled on by myself. Soon afterwards he overtook me at Leephook, where hearing me talk, he knew my voice, called to me, and said, "What, Chandler, are you got so far already?"

"Yes, Sir," said I; "but I am almost tired, and don't care to go any farther tonight."

"No more will I," said he: "but where did you lie last night?"

"Why, Sir, I lay at Kingston."

"So did I," replied he, "and endeavoured to find you out, but could not; and what did you pay for your lodging?"

"Sixpence, Sir," returned I.

"If you had been along with me," said he, "you might have had one for twopence."

We then went to a house and got a beef steak, etc. for supper, and lay there; and the whole expense amounted only to sixteen pence. On asking him what I had to pay, he said, "Nothing." But before we went to bed, the landlady asked if we lay together?

"Yes," said he, "my friend Chandler is a clean lad."

He little knew who he had got to lie with him; I am sure if he had, I should have been otherwise disposed in this respect; for he was always too free among the women.

In the morning we set off, and some time afterwards stopped to refresh ourselves; but he would not suffer me to pay anything: so that I thought I lived very cheap. Though I was lame, and greatly fatigued by this journey, nevertheless I made shift to get to Portsmouth punctually at the time appointed, and soon crossed the water to Gosport.

As soon as I was come to my master's house, my mistress, being in a good humour, gave me some refreshment immediately; and I then told her I had seen Mrs. Cureall's mother at London, and of the civility she shewed me at home and abroad. Whereupon my mistress sent for her; and we had a great deal of conversation together. At night I went to bed, and slept very sound.

In the morning I went to work as usual. But on my return home at night, my mistress was standing at the bar, and Mrs. Cureall with her. Seeing me come in, she said to Mrs. Cureall, "here comes my little curl-pou'd dog; he is ashamed to come and kiss me;" and I can't say but what I was. Upon this I went backwards to consider how I should act, provided she should say so again. After having considered how I should behave myself on this occasion, I went in; and the very moment she saw me return, said, "Why I told you he was ashamed to come and kiss me."

"No, that I am not," said I. Accordingly I went to her; and she stooped down to let me kiss her, when I perceived she was very much in liquor; so that I was obliged to put her to bed, our maid being abed with a young man, who swore next morning that I had been in bed with my mistress. Indeed as I was willing to do anything for a quiet life, it was no wonder that such reports prevailed among the people; though they all agreed that I acted quite right.

But I must here acknowledge with truth, that the frequent quarrels and fighting between my master and mistress made my life very uncomfortable. Their differences and skirmishes were so often repeated, that I was obliged to take a tinderbox in my room to strike a light upon occasion, and go down to part them if I could. One night it happened that I forgot the box; but was obliged to leave my bed on their account, though without light. In groping my way without cloaths on in the street, I stumbled upon a door that was ajar, where I perceived the glimmering of a candle upon the mantle-piece, which I was going to take, not thinking any person was near; when on a sudden a woman entered the room, and cried out, "What the devil do you do here naked?"

I begged of her not to stop me, because I was in a hurry: and have often since thought it was a great mercy I was not found out, that being a very bad house: and it was still a greater wonder that the woman did not take hold of me.

I had no sooner got within doors than I found my mistress with her head out of the window, crying, "Murder," as loud as she could bawl, with the children all in tears about her; which frightened me very much, my master appealing to me as a witness if he was beating her; for he lay at the same time in his bed laughing at her. When she was grown tired on this howling fit, I asked her if she would go to bed, and not alarm the people by these uproars? On which, she said, "Oh the dog! I'll pull out his guts!"

"Come," said I, "will you go to some other bed, and take no father notice of him tonight?"

But it was all to no purpose; since the more I talked to her the worse she was, and the greater noise she made. At length, I got her upstairs, and put her into another bed, where she lay pretty quiet till the morning.

137

I was indeed very glad when the morning came, that I might go to the dock to my work, because there I was free from noise. However, the men used to tell me, out of a sort of waggery, that they would have my mistress and me taken up for common disturbers.

"I wish you would," said I, "for then I should have some peace."

Some time after this, when I came home at night from the dock-yard, I found the maid was going away; and my master being gone over the water, my mistress, who was pretty much intoxicated, put on her hat and cloak, and would forsooth cross the water to find him, which she did at the sign of the Fountain in Portsmouth. The first salute she generally gave him, was a great blow with the first thing she could meet with; which put him into such a passion, that he rose up and beat her in such a violent manner with a stick, that he left her almost lifeless.

Soon after this fray, my mistress came home, where she found me reading my book, and rocking the cradle. On observing her countenance, I perceived she had two black eyes; so that I immediately concluded she had been after my master for something. She then asked me if he was come home? I told her, "No." Whereupon she loaded him with the most reproachful names her imagination could suggest; and afterwards went abroad again.

She had not been gone long before my master came home, and asked if my mistress was come? I told him, she had been at home, but was gone. Whereupon he took a candle, hammer, and nails, went up to his bedchamber, and nailed the door up, to prevent her coming to bed to him.

He had not been in bed long before she came back; and then I apprehended I should have no sleep that night; for I found the old trade was going on again. She asked, If my master was come in? I answered, "Yes."

"Oh the dog!" said she, "I'll pull him out of his bed; for he shall have no rest here this night;" and upstairs she flew. But finding the door was fast, she came down immediately in a great fury for something to break it open, but met with nothing, as I had taken care to put everything out of her reach; for she would take the first thing that came to hand. By some means or other she at length got a scrubbing brush, with which she soon broke a piece out of the door, and then sat down looking through it, saying, "Now I can see you, I am content." But she had not sat long before she got up and fell to work again, till she had demolished the door so far as to make room enough to go in herself; but was afraid to sit down. Having thus done, she went and brought up the young child; and getting upon her knees, first put the child in at the door, and afterwards entered herself. This being done, she threw the child (which was only about two months old) at him: so that I was very much afraid she had killed it. I ran down to fetch the cradle to put the child in, and there sat till three o'clock; all which time they continued fighting; sometimes one getting the better, and sometimes the other; during the whole of which encounter I was obliged to see fair play, though murder should be the consequence. These contests frequently happened, till it was time for me to go to work; and I was very glad to be out of their way; besides, the children were ever crying after me: and it gave me great concern to think the mother should have so little regard for her family, as to neglect them in the manner she did. However, I have some reason to believe the fault was equally chargeable on the husband.

Though I was not turned over to another master, I could not get quite clear of my former; for when I came from the dock, my mistress would make me clean shoes, knives and forks, and do all the drudgery of the house as before. But I had sometimes the courage to tell her, that I was not put 'prentice to be treated in such a manner: with that she catched me by the hair of the head, and turned me out of doors; which the people observing, asked if she was not ashamed to use me in such a rough manner? She said, I should not come there again; though it was excessive cold weather, and I had no friend to go to. Upon this, I went to the taphouse at the Red Lyon, and told the woman in what manner my mistress had served me, and that I would not go there any more if I could help it, though I had no money to pay for a lodging. The woman then told me I should lay there.

On going to work next day, I told the men in the yard in what manner I had been handled by my mistress. They bid me go to the man that I was turned over to, and ask him for my board wages, he being (they said) the only fit person to apply to. Next day I went and told him my case. Whereupon he directed me to come the following day, and he would send his brother over to Mr. Aulquier's, which he did. But Mr. Aulquier would not agree to give me board wages; saying, That if I would not come home and board, he would do nothing more for me. During this time I was obliged to shift as well as I could: But my mistress sent all over the town to find me out, in order to get me back again; however, I took care she should not meet with me.

Soon after this, I went to the Common, to see one Mrs. Reading, who knew me very well when I was on board the *Sandwich*; and asked me in a very friendly manner how I did? I began with telling her how my mistress had served me, by turning me out of doors. She immediately said, "You shall live with me," and that she would engage to get my board wages. Hereupon I went over to Gosport, and related the matter to the woman, telling her where I was going to live, and thanked her for my lodging. She said, I was very welcome; for while I lay there I had a sailor for my bedfellow, and I was glad when I parted from him.

After this I returned to the Common, and lay with Mrs. Readings eldest son, who had no suspicion of my being a woman; and I lived with her as one of her own children; and the man I was turned over to promised me my board wages: on which I thought myself happy.

I shall now present the reader with a letter I sent to my father and mother, as follows:—

Gosport, Feb. 2, 1768.

Hond. Father and Mother,
This comes with my duty to you both, hoping these few lines will find you in good health, as I am at present, thanks be to God for it. Your last letter I received very safe; and am glad to find my mother is so well recovered. Since I wrote to you, I have been turned over to another master, one Mr. Bedworth, who lives upon the Common. My kind love to my brother and sister, and all friends that know me. So conclude with my duty and prayers for you both, from
Your dutiful daughter,

Mary Lacy,

N.B. Please to direct for me thus,
To William Chandler, at the King of Prussia's Head, in Gosport.

To resume my former narrative. My master being returned home from the kings-bench, they were very solicitous for me to come home again; which I would not consent to till my friend Mrs. Reading was satisfied for my board and lodging, which they promised should be paid, as soon as they received some money due to them from a sailor, who at that time was on the other side the water, in Portsmouth town. In order the more speedily to obtain it, they employed an officer to arrest him. But he being well known, they were afraid to go into the houses to look after him; and therefore came home, and said he could not be found.

My mistress then asked me if I would go with her in search of him (which was to be the night following)? To this I the more readily consented, as I was very desirous my friend should have her money. Accordingly next night we went over to the Naked Boy at Portsmouth, and there found him playing at bowls. My mistress then went up to him, and asked if he would drink? whilst I went to call the bailiff's follower: but before I could return, he decamped. She cried out, "Stop thief," with the follower after her: nevertheless, he got clear off for that time.

Soon after, we went in search of him again; and among the number of people we saw, I met with the boatswain's mate of the *Sandwich*, who stared at me, and asked what brought me out at that time of night? I told him I was looking for a particular person, but could not find him; and asked him if there were any other people in the house? To which he answered, there were some upstairs. I then called the bailiff, went upstairs, and found him in bed with a girl, with his face very bloody. We pulled him out of bed, and carried him to Gosport. Mr. Aulquier was gone to bed; however, we soon obliged him to get up, and secured the person we were in quest of. But, notwithstanding all the pains and fatigue I had been at in this troublesome affair, my poor landlady did not recover any of the money due to her, the man being insolvent.

We began now to live at the same poor rate as heretofore, having sometimes had victuals, and at other times none. At length my master gave me two-pence a day for a dinner; and indeed I could not well have less. However, by some fortunate means or other, I used to procure a dinner; so I reserved that two-pence for other uses.

My Master was now become so poor, that he was not able to buy me a pair of shoes: and though at this time it was very cold wet weather, I was obliged to go almost barefooted. However, to make things a little more comfortable, when I went home at night, I used to wash my stockings, and dry them before the fire, to be as comfortable as I could the next day. I had no money to purchase second-hand shoes, which if I had had, they would not have lasted long; and as for shirts, I was obliged to go on trust for them, till I could pay. But I always took care to discharge what I owed for one thing before I bought another; and that was the way I got my cloaths.

The next day I went to the dock, it was whispered about that I was a woman; which threw me into a most terrible fright, believing that some of the boys were going to search me. It was now much about breakfast-time; when coming on shore, in order to go to my chest for my breakfast, two men of our company called, and said, they wanted to speak to me. I went to them. "What think you, Chandler, the people will have it that you are a woman!" which struck me with such a panic that I knew not what to say. However, I had the presence of mind to laugh it off, as if it was not worth notice.

On going to my chest again, I perceived several apprentices waiting, who wanted to search me: but I took care not to run, lest that should increase their suspicion. Hereupon, one Mr. Penny, of our company, came up, and asked them what they meant by surrounding me in that manner? telling them at the same time, that the first person that offered to touch me, he would not only well drub him, but carry him before the builder afterwards, which made them all sheer off; and they were from that time afraid of molesting me any more.

I now sat down, and gave full vent to my tears, which were not few: but the men that I worked with, were gone to breakfast, and knew nothing of the matter till they came back; when my friends thus accosted them, "What think you of your man now?"

"Why, 'tis no such thing," said the others, "and I'll wager you any money upon it;" which made me glad to think they gave it such a turn.

However, when I had done work, the man whose name was Corbin, and his mate that taught me my business, came and told me in a serious manner, I must go with them to be searched; "for if you don't said they, you will be over-hauled by the boys."

Indeed I knew not what to do in this case: but I considered they were very sober men, and that it was safer to trust them than expose myself to the rudeness of the boys. They put the question very seriously, which I as ingenuously answered, though it made me cry so that I could scarce speak; at which declaration of mine, in plainly telling them I was a woman, they seemed greatly surprised; and offered to take their oaths of secrecy.

When they went back, the people asked them if it was true what they had heard? "No," said they, "he is a man and a half to a great many." "Ay," said one, "I thought Chandler could not be so great with his mistress if he was not a man; I'm sure she would not have brought him to the point if he was not so:" and another said, "I'm sure he's no girl; if he was, he would not have gone after so many for nothing, and would have soon been found out."

From such talk as this among the men, in a day or two the matter quite dropped: yet now and then they would say, I wonder how it should come into the heads of the people to think that Chandler was a girl: I am sure there is not the least appearance of it in the make or shape of him. Indeed Mr. Corbin never gave the least hint or token of such a suspicion, any more than if he had not known or thought any thing of the matter: nor could I discover or conceive, at the time, what gave rise to this extraordinary affair, or by what means it could take wind about the yard. My girl at Gosport had heard it, but could not believe it. She believed I had received every favour, and taken every freedom that could be practised by the gallants, or she would not have given her company to me, though at this time I was not so very intimate with her as heretofore.

I must now return to my old lady, who was going to remove to another house; so that there was no space for me to lie in, which obliged me to go home to my masters house, who had lately hired a new servant. I was to lie in the fore garret, and she in the back one. Mr. Aulquier lay below; but I had some suspicion they lay together, though I never heard her go up or downstairs. However, when I went down one morning, I overheard them talking, which confirmed me in the opinion that they were bedfellows. It grieved me to think what ruin the girl was bringing upon herself; and therefore thought it my duty to tell her of it, which I did when I came home to dinner, though she denied it: but when I came to tax her with what passed betwixt them, she could not help owning it to me. Whereupon I advised her to leave him. She said, She did not know what to do.

And I should have been heartily glad if she had quitted the place; for she used me very ill, by dashing my milk with water at supper, and then charging the fault upon another. And at dinner time, when they had duck, fowl, or any fine roast meat, they would frequently send me away with a piece of bread and cheese, by saying that dinner would not be dressed time enough for me. But she soon afterwards began to use me better, being afraid I should go and inform her mother of her behaviour. The following Sunday Mr. Aulquier and she fell out, and had a scuffle together; and in the fray she tore off his shirtsleeves, and then went out of doors. So that there being nobody to dress the dinner but me, I put on the pot with some pork and greens, which was a good meal for me. But he soon prevailed on her to come back again.

It will be necessary here to make some farther mention of my old mistress, who still lived along with Mr. ——r. She took no thought or concern about her children, and was alike neglectful of herself, owing to her turbulent and furious disposition: for after she had lived with Mr. A——r but a short time, she cut his head and hand with a quart pot, which provoked him to send her to Bridewell for her good behaviour. While she was there, her mother desired me to carry a letter to her, which I said I would do, provided she first obtained my master's consent; which he readily granted. Upon bringing her the letter, she said, "Bill, what do you think I dreamt of last night?"

"I don't know," said I.

"Why," says she, "I dreamt that you and I were married."

"Oh then," replied I, "you will have a good husband when you have me."

Whereupon she called for a pot of beer, to drink with her: she then read the letter, the contents of which gave her a better opinion of herself; and afterwards asked me if I would go to Mr. Rimes, the man she had lived with, and endeavour to prevail upon him to procure her release.

I told her I would, which I accordingly did; when he began with telling in what manner she had used him.

"Well," said I, "you have put her in, and you must take her out again."

He replied, "I know I must; and this I know also, that all the people will think me an arrant fool for so doing; however, you may let her know, that she shall be discharged tomorrow."

I went immediately and told the mother and her what I had done in the matter. The mother was glad to hear of my success in it; but desired (though she was her child) that she would not come near her again.

To return to my old sweetheart Sarah. The next day when I was going from work, she came up to the dockyard, and asked me if I would go along with her to a christening? After a short pause, I told her I did not care to stand for the child. Whereupon she went and gave the people notice of my dislike to the proposal, who took care to provide a godfather in my room. But notwithstanding my refusal to answer for the child, I could not be excused from going with her to the house: so that when I came from the dock after dinner, I was obliged to lose half a day's work to please her. We were very merry together: everything was conduced in tolerable order; and we broke up in good time, which gave me an opportunity of seeing her home; which caused a report to be spread all over the town, that we were going to be married next day; and there were many that believed it. For my part I was glad that I was so near the expiration of my time, because I should then be my own master; for I still went to Mr. L——'s, and met with a very good sort of gentlewoman who lived there. She asked me if I went to church? I told her, yes, when I had an opportunity.

She afterwards gave me many useful admonitions, which disposed me to be very thankful to God for his goodness, in protecting me amidst the many dangers I had brought upon myself: and I flattered myself that I should some time or other be enabled to make amends to my parents for all the trouble I had brought upon them. But the worst embarrassment I had involved myself in, was my being so intimate with Sarah. Indeed I had almost taken a resolution to break off correspondence, not only with Sarah, but even with every one of those with whom I had contracted an acquaintance of that sort; for I found it almost impossible to free myself from their importunities any other way.

I considered it as a very surprising event that Mrs. Low should pretend to have such a regard for my interest, and at length betray me. She told me, I should be welcome to come and lodge with her, when I was out of my time; and by continually repeating this profession of her kindness towards me, I thought she was the best friend I had; for I could not form the least idea of her being so deceitful as to discover me, after she had given my mother an absolute promise to the contrary. Indeed I esteemed myself happy in having met with a person I could freely unbosom myself to, being perfectly satisfied of her fidelity; on which account I really thought I could not make her a too grateful return; which consideration often induced me to carry her a bundle of chips.

I shall now proceed to the concluding scenes of my folly. Being but very indifferently accommodated in regard to cloathing, my master aggravated my distress, by not permitting me to receive the three pounds a year; neither would he procure me any apparel, though the money was regularly paid him: and, notwithstanding he enjoyed every advantage he could possibly expect, yet was so unkind as to refuse me even a pair of shoes, when I was barefooted. On the day before my time expired, being at work upon the *Pallas* frigate, Sarah came and invited me to breakfast with her the next morning, which I did. Having afterwards cleaned myself, I went to the builder's office, and told him, it was the last day of my time, and hoped he had no objection against my certificate being allowed me. On asking to whom I served my time? I told him. He then called his clerk, and ordered him to prepare my certificate, which he accordingly did; after which, I went to each of the proper persons, who readily signed it. I then carried the certificate to the clerk of the cheques office, where I was entered as a man.

After this I went to reside upon the Common, as I supposed it would be most satisfactory to my mother. I lived there as retired as I could, and kept to my work. Soon after which, the company that I belonged to were ordered to go and break up an old ship that lay in the dock: but we found it very hard to demolish her; and I likewise found the labour much too hard for me, though I never gave out; for at the best of times the work was very fatiguing. But the money we earned was acceptable to me, since having owed some during my apprenticeship, I was glad to have it in my power to pay everyone as fast as I could: and, beside, I was willing, if I could, to make a creditable appearance.

Being now out of my time, I resolved to send down for my mother to come to me, believing it to be best for both, that no time might be lost. So I wrote the following letter to my parents:

Portsmouth, May 15, 1770.

Hond. Father and Mother,

I hope these few lines will find you both in perfect health, as I am at present, thanks be to God for it. I have the pleasure to let you know I am out of my time, and live along with Mrs. Low, and shall be very glad if you will come down and see me; which if you are inclined to do, pray write me word, and my answer shall contain directions for the best road you are to take. Pray give my kind love to my brother and sister, and all friends that know me. I conclude, with my prayers to God for you both,

your dutiful daughter,

Mary Lacy.

P.S. Direct to me as follows:

To William Chandler, at Mrs. Low's, in the Tree Rope-Walk, Portsmouth Common.

Next day as I lay in my bed, I heard the dock-bell ring, on which I got up, and dressed myself as fast as I could, lest I should be too late to the call. But notwithstanding the haste I made, the bell still kept ringing, which raised my wonder at the reason it rang so long. As soon as

I came up to the dock-wall I met a boatswain running with his coat off, which made me conclude something very extraordinary was the matter. When I came up to the dock gate, I found that all the yard was in a blaze, and the engines getting out; for the fire was so great and powerful that its heat almost resembled that of a furnace: and I think I never in my life suffered so much for want of drink, as I did during the hurry and confusion it occasioned; the yard and taphouse being crowded with people, there was no getting any liquor.

While the fire was burning, a quarterman was dispatched to London with an account of it; and I was appointed to guard his house till he returned. After it was extinguished, we had orders to work a day and two tides; and were in a very great hurry at Portsmouth. The reason why I left Mrs. Low was, because, after taking her for my friend, I at length discovered she had been all along the greatest enemy I ever had, having done many pitiful mean actions to me; but the betraying me exceeded all the rest, and was almost equal to the depriving me of life. It is most certain, she was an inveterate enemy to me, which she evidenced by endeavouring to do me all this disservice in her power, and that at a time when I was not possessed of a penny of money in the world, which I could call my own.

However, all other injuries I should have regarded but little, if she had not discovered me to the men; for when Mrs. F——s told me what I was, I fretted myself quite sick, and thought I should have broke my heart; but could not tell who she had told: and the apprehensions I felt from persons meddling with me, greatly affected me. So that by fretting and hard working, I was reduced very low, and thrown into a fit of illness; which those people who were ignorant of the real cause, construed to be love.

About this time an order came down for us to leave off working double tides, and only to work one day and two tides, which I was not sorry for; particularly on one account, as I was almost spent with working so close; for in a little time afterwards, I was served with so bad a swelling in my thighs that I was not able to walk, and was unwilling the doctor should look at it, lest he should find me out: I therefore sent for the quarterman to answer for me that I was sick; which he accordingly did; and I continued a week before I was able to go into the yard again, and was then incapable of doing any work.

In a short time after I became better, and resumed my labour; after which we were ordered to go to Spithead to work, where we were in as bad a situation as before, having no other place to lie on but the softest plank we could find: so that such a wretched accommodation during that time made me catch cold again in my thighs, and occasioned my illness to return; however, I soon mended. But as the people were shifted about from one company to another, on the first of April I became very uneasy, less something disastrous should happen to me.

A short time after this, I was, on account of lameness, forced to go upon the doctor's list for a fortnight: but thank God I got the better of this, and went to work again, though continually apprehensive of being surprised unawares; for I did not know the particular persons my false friend had betrayed me to.

Soon afterwards our company was ordered to tear up an old forty gun ship, which was so very difficult to take to pieces that I strained my loins in an attempt; the effects of which I felt very sensibly at night when I went home, for I could hardly stand; and had no appetite to my victuals. But, notwithstanding my legs would scarce support me, I continued working till the ship was quite demolished, and then we were ordered on board the *Sandwich*, to bring on her waleing, which was very heavy.

This increased my weakness to such a degree, that the going to work proved very irksome to me, insomuch that every body wondered what was the matter: however, I still continued my labour, till want of strength obliged me to quit it; and then I went to the doctors shop, and told him I had strained my loins, which disabled me from working. Whereupon he gave me something which he thought would relieve me. I took it; but had it not been for the infinite mercy of God towards me, I should certainly have been killed by it, the medicine being altogether improper for my complaint; in consequence whereof, instead of growing better, I became every day worse than the former, which made me think I could not live long. However, in process of time my complaint abated, but not so as to enable me to work as I had done before, nor could I carry the same burdens as usual, which made me very uneasy.

While I continued in this weak condition, I imagined that if I could go down to Kent I might get a friend to help me out of the yard: but growing somewhat better, I went to work as well as I could. The loss of my father and mother like-wife greatly aggravated my concern; and I began to think of endeavouring to obtain liberty of the builder to go into Kent for a fortnight, which he readily granted. I went accordingly in one of the transports to Dover, from thence to Ash, and afterwards to the house of Mrs. Deverton, who was very much surprised at seeing me, and told me she had been up to London last week; and that her brother and sister at Kensington would be glad to see me.

On hearing this, I took my leave of Ash and set off for London; and when I came to Deptford, I met with William L——y, who was glad to see me. I told him I had got a letter for him from Betty S——e. I went home, and lay all night with him; for as I had done so before, I was not afraid of him. Having talked much to him about his girl, the next day he went with me to London; for I wanted to go to the Navy Office to get my liberty prolonged, where they told me I must come again some other day.

From the Navy Office my companion went with me to Kensington: but when I came there, I was apprehensive Mr. Richardson would betray me to the young man who did not know what I was: to prevent which, I immediately enquired for the gentleman's house; which being directed to, the people belonging to it informed me that he lived there; but I did not know any of them, as it was seventeen years since I had seen them before.

I told Mrs. Richardson that I had brought her a letter from Ash; and almost as soon as she had looked on it, she recollected who I was: but I desired her to be careful what she said before the young man, otherwise it would be the means of betraying me. She strictly complied with my request till he was gone. This was on Thursday; and I staid there until the Sunday night following, then set off; for I did not know that my liberty was renewed at the Navy Office. I got to Portsmouth on Monday; and I immediately informed the builder I was come back. Whereupon he told me that my liberty was renewed. However, I went to work; but was in a short time after taken as ill as ever.

As soon as I heard that Mrs. Low had told everybody who I was, I was ready to break my heart; and immediately wrote to Mr. Richardson at Kensington, to desire him, if possible, to assist me. He sent me word he could not do anything for me at that time, because all the gentlemen were out of town; but that in a months time he would write, and let me know farther.

I endeavoured to keep up my spirits under these discouragements as well as I could; but still found the work proved harder and more fatiguing to me: Nor had I been from London a month before I was entered to the doctor's lift; for we had been putting the *Sandwich* in thorough repair, the working on which gave me such a pain in my side, that I was obliged to have a blister applied to it; and though the doctor's mate dressed it every day, he never discovered that I was a woman but often asked me why I did not marry.

In this condition I continued for some time; during which Mrs. Low came from Woolwich. The very mention of this traitorous woman's name made me worse (for three or four days) than I was before. She had been but a short time in Portsmouth before Mr. Richardson sent for me to come up to Kensington; for as they new my father and mother, they were very much concerned about my welfare. This news in a few days gave a happy turn to my disorder, and almost restored me to health: so that I embraced the first opportunity of going over to Gosport, to take leave of them all; and went directly home to make myself ready to go with the coach.

My parting with the young women occasioned a scene of great perplexity and distress; and indeed one of them was ready to break her heart. This was poor Sarah, whose pitiable case affected me very much. However, I set off from Portsmouth the second day of December, 1771, and reached Kensington the next day; when Mr. Richardson advised me that the best step I could take was, to present a petition to the lords of the admiralty; which I accordingly did: and, their lordships, in consideration of my extraordinary sufferings and services, circumstanced as I was, have been so generous as to settle 20*l*. a year upon me: for which, as in gratitude and duty bound, I shall pray for them as long as I live.

After the lords of the admiralty had granted my superannuated pension, I continued with the above mentioned Mr. Richardson as Kensington for about the space of ten months, during which time, on going to Deptford to receive my money, I was met by one Mr. Slade, who had removed thither from Portsmouth yard by order of the board. He has not seen me before in women's apparel; yet having heard of my metamorphosis, he enquired kindly after my health, and offered his service to conduct me back to Kensington.

On the road thither, he expressed a great affection for me; and at the same time requested me to give him my hand at the altar, allowing me a proper time to consider of his offer. Though I had repeatedly declared that I would remain single, yet afterwards having the utmost reason to believe that there subsisted a real and mutual affection betwixt us, and that the hand of Providence was engaged in bringing about our union, I at length gave my consent; in consequence of which, we were married, and now enjoy the utmost happiness the state affords; which I have the most sanguine hopes of a continuance of, since my husband is not only sober and industrious, but having been convinced, ever since the year 1762, of the important truths of Christianity, his conduct towards mankind in general, founded on a love of virtue, is upright and exemplary; at the same time that in his conjugal relation he behaves in the most endearing and indulgent manner. Thus united, I have, by the blessing of God, attained more than a bare chance for happiness in my present state, and have also the most solid grounds to look for the permanent enjoyment of it in future.

Anna Maria Real
Amelia Opie (*Memoirs* account)

When I was scarcely yet in my teens, a highly respected friend of mine, a member of the Society of Friends, informed me that she had a curious story to relate to me and her niece, my favourite friend and companion; she told us that her husband had received a letter from a friend at Lynn, recommending to his kindness a young man, named William Henry Renny, who was a sailor, just come on shore from a distant part, and wanted some assistance on his way (I think) to London. My friend, who was ever ready to lend his aid when needed, and was sure his correspondent would not have required it for one unworthy, received the young man kindly, and ordered him refreshments in the servants hall; and, as I believe, prepared for him a bed in his own house. But before the evening came, my friend had observed something in the young man's manner which he did not like; he was too familiar towards the servants, and certainly did not seem a proper inmate for the family of a Friend.

At length, in consequence of hints given him by someone in the family, he called the stranger into his study, and expressed his vexation at learning that his conduct had not been quite correct. The young man listened respectfully to the deserved rebuke, but with great agitation and considerable excitement, occasioned perhaps, as my candid friend thought, by better meals than he had been used to, and which was therefore a sort of excuse for his behaviour; but little was my friend prepared for the disclosure that awaited him. Falling on his knees, the young man, with clasped hands, conjured his hearer to forgive him the imposition he had practised. "Oh, sir," cried he, "I am an impostor, my name is not William Henry R. but Anna Maria Real, I am not a man, but a woman!"

Such a confession would have astounded anyone; judge then how it must have affected the correct man whom she addressed! who certainly did not let the woman remain in her abject position, but desired immediately to hear a true account of who and what she was. She said, that her lover, when very young, had left her to go to sea, and that she resolved to follow him to Russia, whither he was bound; that she did follow him, disguised as a sailor, and had worked out her passage undetected. She found her lover dead, but she liked a sailor's life so well, that she had continued in the service up to that time, when (for some reason which I have forgotten) she left the ship, and came ashore at Lynn, not meaning to return to it, but to resume the garb of her sex. On this latter condition, my friend and his wife were willing to assist her, and endeavour to effect a reformation in her. The first step was to procure her a lodging that evening, and to prevent her being seen, as much as they could, before she had put on woman's clothes. Accordingly, she was sent to lodgings, and inquiries into the truth of her story were instituted at Lynn and elsewhere.

But what an interesting tale was this for me, a Miss just entered into her teens! Of a female soldier's adventures I had some years previously heard, and once had seen Hannah Snell,[1] a native of Norfolk, who had followed her lover to the wars. Here was a female sailor added to my experience. Every opportunity of hearing any subsequent detail was eagerly seized. What a romantic incident! The romance of real life too! How I wanted to see the heroine; and I was rather mortified that my sober-minded friend would not describe her features to me.

"Might I," I asked, "be at last allowed to see her?" and as my parents gave leave, I, accompanied by a young friend, called at the adventurer's lodgings, who was at home! Yes, she was at home, and to our great consternation we found her in men's clothes still, and working at a trade which she had acquired on board ship, the trade of a tailor! Nor did she leave off though we were her guests, but went on stitching and pulling with most ugly diligence, though ever and *anon* casting her large, dark, and really beautiful, though fierce eyes, over our disturbed and wondering countenances, silently awaiting to hear why we came.

We found it difficult to give a reason, as her appearance and employment so totally extinguished any thing like sentiment in our young hearts, upon this occasion. However, we broke the ice at last,

1. *The Female Soldier,* two accounts of women who served & fought as men, *The Female Soldier; or, the Surprising Life and Adventures of Hannah Snell* by Hannah Snell and *Frances Scanagatti or, the Female Soldier* by Anonymous is also published by Leonaur.

and she told us something of her story; which, however touching in the beginning, as that of a disguise and an enterprise prompted by youthful love, became utterly offensive when persisted in after the original motives for it had ceased. Her manner too was not pleasant: I wore a gold watch in my girdle, with a smart chain and seals, and the coveting eye with which she gazed, and at length clapped her hand upon them, begging to see them near, gave me a feeling of distaste; and, as I watched her almost terrible eyes, I fancied that they indicated a deranged mind; therefore, hastening to give her the money which I had brought for her, I took my leave, with my friend, resolving not to visit her again. Out of respect to our friends, she went to the Friends meeting with them, and they were pleased to see her there in her woman's attire; but when she walked away, with the long strides and bold seeming of a man, it was anything rather than satisfactory, to observe her.

I once saw her walk, and though this romance of real life occupied the minds of my young friend and myself, and was afterwards discussed by us, still the actress in it was be coming, justly, an object with whom we should have loathed any intercourse.

I do not recollect how long she remained under the care of my excellent friends, but I think much of her story was authenticated by the answers to the inquiries made. All that I know with certainty is, that a collection of wild beasts came to town, the showman of which turned out to be Maria Real's husband, and with him she left Norwich!

I FELL UPON MY KNEES AND BESOUGHT HIM TO SPARE ME, A POOR
FRIENDLESS ORPHAN.

The Life and Sufferings of Miss Emma Cole
Written by Herself

Reader,—dispensing with an introduction, I will enter at once upon the history of my *Life and Sufferings*; and although in many cases it may afford us but little satisfaction in taking a retrospective glance of our past life, yet with myself it is a source of much real pleasure to turn over the pages in the volume of events of my chequered life, treasured in my memory, and to thank the great Author of my being, who has carried me safely through so many trying scenes.

I was born in the State of Maine. And although my parents were poor, they were honest. My father gained a livelihood for his family by cultivating a small piece of land, and occasionally fishing. Being the only child of my parents I was their idol. Beneath their parental roof I lived in my innocence, happy and contented, and sorrow was a stranger to my buoyant heart. I would that the conscious delights of those days had never departed from me; but alas! my father became a prey to a consumption, and then could perform but little labour; and it was with much difficulty my poor mother could support us, I being quite young, then only about five years of age.

For two years previous my father grew worse; at last he paid the debt of nature. His loss preyed on my mother, and threw her into a fever, and she survived him only about three months and then she too left me, giving me the best of advice. It was a solemn time for me, and I shall never forget the grief of my little bosom at that moment when she closed her eyes in death. I said within myself, would that I could have died for her. Alas! I was now left alone to drift upon the wide waters of the world, having neither house nor home; for the premises improved by my parents were only hired, and the little personal property they had went to defray the expenses of sickness.

Being poorly clad, I hardly knew where to wander; but an old friend of my father's, by the name of Smith, offered me an opportunity to come and live in. his family. I immediately embraced the opportunity, and was treated well, but it did not seem like my father's house. I had to do the drudgery for all the family; that I was willing to do, even anything that lay in my power, to make them satisfied and contented.

Time passed on, and I found myself in my fourteenth year. It was my study to make all around me happy and contented. I very seldom left to go anywhere, except to church, and there I could go but seldom, most always on Sundays having to take care of the children, in order that the family might attend. I remained quite happy, until a young man in the neighbourhood, by the name of Hackley, one day as the rest of the family were away from home, came to the house. Standing high in the estimation of this world, having rich parents and relations, and being quite handsome, he thought that all must obey him at his request or command.

As soon as he was aware that I was alone, and knowing also that I was a poor orphan, he conceived the thought of robbing me of all that makes life valuable—character. But I resisted to the utmost of my strength and abilities; and I succeeded in frustrating his fiendish schemes. After this I left the house, and fled to one of the nearest neighbours, intending to expose him; but as I arrived there, I found the family were engaged with some newly arrived friends, and therefore I concluded to defer it until a more convenient time. I stopped there a short time and returned home. The family had just arrived a few moments before me, but they also had brought with them some of their friends, and I had not an opportunity to expose the villain. I immediately went about my customary employments, and in a few hours there came two persons to the house, who desired to speak privately with Mr. and Mrs. Smith, and they all went into another room by themselves.

As they spoke rather loud, I could perceive that Mr. and Mrs. Smith were quite angry, but could understand only a little that was said; I heard my name several times repeated. At last they came out and went into several rooms, and then I was taken aside, and totally confounded by the declaration, that I had stolen and secreted their silver spoons. I declared upon my honour I had not taken them. They said that I was an imposter, that I was not to be believed, and that I had broken several locks, and taken articles not belonging to me, some of which were secreted in my trunk. I resolutely denied every charge, but was told, that as they had detected my dishonesty, I must quit their house, for they could no longer harbour an imposter. I fell on my knees at their feet, and called heaven to witness that I was innocent of the dreadful charges they had made, and implored them not to cast me off; but their hearts appeared as hard as adamant; they said they would not listen to any words, for they had caught me already in several falsehoods, and therefore would hear nothing more from me; and giving me my bonnet and shawl, desired me to quit their house immediately, and never let them see me again.

I arose with a bursting heart, and made my way out of the house. I wandered a few steps, and fainted. When I revived, it was with much difficulty that I could convince myself but that it was a dream; but alas, I soon found that it was reality. I wandered about until it was quite dark. Not knowing whither I had strayed, I came to a miserable looking hut and knocked at the door. An old lady came to the door and wished to know what I wanted. I told her that I had lost my way, and did not know where I was, and inquired how far it was to Mr. Smith's. She told me it was about five miles, and asked me to walk in. I was glad of the invitation, for it had been raining most of the afternoon, and I had got completely drenched.

I was glad even to find this shelter, although it was a wretched looking place. There stood a small pine table in the middle of the floor, and on it a candle and a few roasted potatoes, and a little cold meat; without bread, cakes, pie or tea. In the fireplace were a few embers. The woman seeing that I was quite wet, immediately built a good fire and I sat down by it. I could not help thinking of my situation. She saw that I was much embarrassed, and invited me to her supper table. I thankfully accepted her invitation. After supper she made a bed for me before the fire, and laying myself down, I could not sleep, my mind being so much affected by my situation.

At last I fell into a profound slumber, and did not awake until aroused by the old lady's preparations for breakfast, which was a very meagre affair, but of which I partook with her. She then wished to know how I happened to get lost. I now informed her of my situation; she sympathized with me much. I could not conceive how those articles came in my trunk, unless that villain had placed them there to ruin me; the old lady thought that his intention in pursuing this course was to drive me from the town to save his own reputation. I did not know what to do or where to go; it would not do for me to stay here and live on the old lady, for she had told me her situation. She was once rich and happy; her husband lost his fortune in the last war, which worried him so that it threw him into a consumption, and he died, leaving her nearly penniless. Her friends almost entirely forgot her, and very seldom called on her, and in but few instances offered her the least assistance.

She was much surprised at their cool treatment, and therefore chose to retire from their society, rather than to be so neglected by them; so she obtained this hovel of a place, and had supported herself here by her own industry. "It is true, I have fared hard," she said, "but I have not had to be dependent on any of my pretended friends, or those that I considered my true friends, when kind providence filled our storehouses to overflowing; but who, when misfortunes came on me, fled and left me to wander alone." The old lady wished me to remain longer, but I could not consent, knowing that it would take from her small pittance, which she had provided for a long cold winter; so I took my leave of her. She gave me good advice, and warned me to take heed of my character, for one false step might precipitate me in the deepest abyss of misery; that I must expect to find a rough and uneven path to tread, at the best.

In return, I declared that no temptation could shake my resolution, or make me swerve from the paths of rectitude. She seemed much pleased to find that I resolved to lean to virtue's side, even at the hazard of my life. I thanked her much for her kindness, for truly the poor widow's mite was much to me. Having left her hospitable roof, I determined to set out on foot for Bangor, and arrived there after a day's journey, much fatigued. Being now penniless, I had to beg the favour in an obscure house of a night's lodging.

In the morning I went in quest of employment, and began to think I should find none, when a lady informed me that a female was wanted to attend some ladies on their passage to Boston, and the offer having been made me of the situation, I gladly accepted it. There were several ladies on board, one of whom wished to engage me as a domestic in her house when we should arrive in Boston. I gladly accepted the offer, and on our arrival in Boston, accompanied her to her house. She kindly supplied me with clothes, and did much to make me happy, and while under her roof I felt that I had again a mother.

But a bitter draught was soon to be handed me. I learnt that my best of friends was about to visit Europe, to be absent for a few years;

consequently, my services were not wanted any longer. Before her departure she presented me with clothing, and procured me another place at service. The name of the family where I now went to live was Haden. At this place my duties were very arduous, but I bore them as well as I could, being supported by that innate sense of rectitude which has ever accompanied me, and feeling a sense of satisfactory pride, that I was earning my livelihood, and was not a dependent on others.

I had been at this place about a year, and had not taken up any of my wages; when one day I heard that Haden had become a bankrupt. I then requested a settlement of Mrs. Haden, who informed me that all their effects had been put into the hands of their creditors, and she could not pay me a farthing, and that they were in a few days to break up housekeeping.

Thus I was again obliged to find a home. I took board, and during the time that I was in search of a situation, had to part with every article I could spare of my scanty clothing, to defray the expenses of my board. I daily visited the intelligence offices, but found no suitable place; until one day. I being at the office, an elderly lady alighted from a carriage and stepped into the office. She said she was in search of a girl as a help in her family. She addressed me, and was quite inquisitive as to who and what I was, and where I came from. I replied to her, that I was destitute, and an orphan. She seemed satisfied with my answers, and the wages having been agreed on, she bade me follow her into her carriage, which stopped at a fine looking house in Eliot street, at the south part of the city.

On entering, I observed a number of good looking young ladies, to whom I was introduced as her friends. I was informed that my duty would be to take charge of two or three sleeping apartments. The ladies gave me to understand, that as some gentlemen were to call that evening, I might retire if I chose, but would like to have me present the next evening. I thanked them for the privilege of retiring, and went to bed quite early, for I did not wish to see their company.

On entering my chamber, I closed and made secure the door, then looked beneath the bed and in the closets to see that all was right. Having satisfied myself, I went to bed, and began to recall to my mind the numerous hardships I had gone through, for one so young, and hoping that a better fate awaited me; not dreaming that any fresh misfortunes were near at hand, or but that I was perfectly secure in my new situation. It was quite late when I fell asleep. I had not been asleep long, when I was awakened by voices in an adjoining room; the parties appeared to be angry, and used many oaths, but I could not distinguish what was said. This alarmed me so much that I could not close my eyes in sleep again the remainder of the night. I feared I had got into a house of disreputable character; and I determined to watch every movement, and if I discovered it to be so, to leave it at once. Things seemed to go on smoothly the next day, and on asking one of the girls the occasion of the noise the last night, she told me that the street door having been inadvertently left open that night, a drunken fellow had mistaken his way and entered the house, and this occasioned the noise I had heard. I did not credit this account, but said nothing more about it.

At last, evening came once more, and the old lady told me that a rich young man of her acquaintance, from the South, was expected there that evening, and she desired me to be very attentive to wait on him, and be particular not to displease him, as he was of a passionate temper, and yet was a very fine fellow, and always made presents when he called. I promised to do my duty. In the evening he arrived, and occasionally there came in other young men. I scrutinised their appearance and conduct very narrowly.

After a while the old lady's relative from the South complained of being unwell, and I was desired to show him to an apartment where he might sleep. Having shown him up to his room, I was about to return, when I was seized by him and dragged into his chamber. He then told me it would be useless for me to resist, as I was completely in his power, and gave me the horrible intelligence of the character of the house I was in. I fell on my knees, and begged him to spare a friendless orphan; that I had no knowledge of the kind of house I was in, and implored him to pity me, and let me instantly depart. He replied by laughing, and saying there was no use of whining about it. I could perceive protruding from his vest the handle of a dirk.

Despair now seized me, and while in his grasp, I made a sudden movement and snatched the dagger from his breast; this disengaged him, and I then warned him not to approach me, or I should take his life. He made an attempt to get the weapon from me, but with my whole muscular strength I made a thrust at him, which sent the weapon in to its hilt. He fell, and uttered a deep groan. I quickly unlocked the door, and catching my shawl as I passed down the stairs, made my way out of the house as soon as I could. I expected that I must certainly have killed him, and my feelings can better be imagined than described.

I at once determined to return to the house at which I had been boarding before I was inveigled into that house of abomination. By good luck I easily found it. The door was unlocked, and perceiving company in the house, I went to the room which I had occupied, and retired to bed, trembling, and a cold clammy sweat standing on my face, and scarcely daring to indulge the thought of what had just passed. I soon heard someone coming up to my chamber, and I feigned to be asleep. It was the landlady; she approached and spoke to me. I appeared to awake. She seemed pleased to see me, and wished to know when I returned from my visit. I told her I had returned early that evening, but observing that she had friends to see her, I did not like to intrude, especially as I was a stranger. She supposed I had been on a visit to some friends, and inquired if I enjoyed myself.

I told her I had been rather unwell, and did not enjoy my visit so much as I otherwise should. Making a few more friendly remarks, she bade me goodnight, and I was left to reflect on my miserable situation. Sleep did not close my eyelids that night. It was now evident that my condition was a desperate one, and that my cup of woe was full; I had never before been so miserable. I was at a loss what course to pursue. It was evident that if I had killed the man, the old woman and her *friends* would be witnesses against me, and although it was not known where I had fled, it would be an easy matter to find me. I was consoled by the thought, that if I had killed the man, it was in defence of my honour, which I valued more than life.

A thousand schemes floated in my mind that night; at length, towards morning I conceived the bold idea of exchanging my clothes for a sailor's, and endeavouring to procure the berth of cook on board some vessel, whither bound was of little consequence to me. Having got up, I dressed myself with as little clothing as I could to appear decent, and took the remainder to a cast-off clothing shop, and readily exchanged them. Having procured the sailor's dress, I packed it up snugly and carried it to my lodgings, and went to my chamber, put on the clothes, which fitted me as well as if they had been made for me. I then put on my woman's clothes again, and went to a barber and had my hair cut off, which I sold to him. I then settled with the landlady for my board.

My imagined difficulty now was to get an opportunity to ship on board a vessel. But a chance soon presented itself, as the cook engaged in a certain vessel had been taken sick, I was taken in his place; the wages were to be ten dollars a month, and the voyage to Europe. She sailed on the same day I shipped, and I felt much relieved on quitting Boston, which had been the scene of that awful tragedy, in which I was doomed to play so conspicuous a part. I had not yet seen our captain; the owner and the mate having engaged me. On asking where Captain Gregory was, (that was his name,) I was told that he was on board, but was rather unwell. As we passed the light-houses and were standing out to sea, I overheard the first and second mate conversing about the captain, when one of them observed, that he had got stabbed the night before, by a girl, and mentioned the street and the circumstances.

It was now evident to me, that the captain was the same individual I had encountered at the afore-mentioned house of ill fame. I was confounded again with my extraordinary situation; an evil genius seemed to pursue me. I must now be confined by this demon, and he my master. But desponding would be useless, and I resolved to muster courage, and trust in that kind Providence that had already rescued me from so many impending dangers. I was at first a little seasick, but soon recovered, and went about my work with as much familiarity as I could, and endeavouring to imitate the voice of a man as much as possible.

After we had been out about twenty days, the captain had so far recovered that he appeared upon deck. He did not recognise his intended victim, through my disguise, and often spoke of the girl, and said she had done right, although it had nearly cost him his life. The vessel being old, it was resolved to repair her on her arrival in London. We arrived in port, and the captain gave us leave to quit the vessel's service if we wished, as it would take two or more months time to repair her. For my part I was rejoiced to leave the vessel, which I did at once.

I wandered about the streets of London for about a day, in search of employment, but found none; and my only alternative was to go to sea again. Having procured myself some clothing and other necessary articles, shipped in the brig *Juba*, destined for New Orleans, having been in London ten days. For several days after we left port we had a very fair wind, and nothing unusual occurred to disturb the monotony of the voyage.

One afternoon, we saw a sail at a distance, which was approaching us. At first no fears were entertained in regard to her character; but as she neared us, we began to suspect her. The captain ordered all sail to be hoisted, which was done. We were now commanded to put ourselves in a situation of defence, which we did with the scanty means that the vessel afforded. But the wind springing up, we began to distance her. Night coming on, attended by a squall, we changed our course, and kept no lights to be seen, hoping by this means to elude her. But as morning dawned she was still in sight, and the wind had greatly subsided. She gained on us fast, and about ten o'clock in the forenoon came along, and sent us a broadside salute, which carried away our main-mast. We were now very near one another. We fought with such arms as the vessel afforded, until there were but three souls left alive to defend her. It being useless to contend longer, we ceased, and the vessel being boarded, we expected no quarters.

The pirates, however, after having plundered and scuttled our vessel, and taken us to their own, offered us the alternative of joining their gang, and of swearing faithfulness to them,—or death. Between these we must instantly decide. My two comrades did not long hesitate to join them. In this awful situation, I uttered a fleeting prayer to God for strength to make my decision. Heaven answered my appeal, and enabled me resolutely to declare to the murderers, that I preferred death rather than shed a fellow-being's blood, except in defence of life. This enraged them, and I was dragged by my hair to the yard-arm, and there secured. Why I was not despatched at once I did not know, unless I was reserved for a subject of torture.

They had scarcely finished binding me, when a sudden gust of wind struck the vessel, and laid her on her beam-ends, but she soon resumed her position. A violent storm had been coming on, which now broke upon us with great violence, and which on the second day, had driven us in sight of land, which proved to be an island. Death now stared everyone in the face, which to me was far more welcome than to unite myself with these fiends in the likeness of men, and shed innocent blood for the sake of gold. As the vessel neared the shore, the anchors were thrown out, but the cables parted, and imminent death was before us. The captain ordered me to be unbound, for he said we should all be in eternity soon. I was then unbound. The sea ran very high, but the vessel striking upon a sandy shore, by a kind Providence we were all saved. She soon after went to pieces, and we were left on an apparently desolate island.

The pirates now began to be affected by a different feeling towards me than they had before entertained. The principle of virtue and humanity, which actuated me, seemed to have its benign effects, even on

EMMA, AS A SAILOR, CAPTURED OH THE HIGH SEAS, AND BOUND BY PIRATES.

their flinty and murderous hearts. They were witnesses that I chose death at their hands, rather than steep my own in the warm blood of a fellow being. I treated them kindly, and savage as were their natures, I was used much better than my two former comrades who had joined their gang.

We had not been long in this situation, when we were visited by a small party of Indians, from a neighbouring island. They appeared of a friendly character, and observing we were destitute of provisions, supplied us from their own. A bloody tragedy was again to be enacted by the heartless pirates. The canoes and other articles belonging to the Indians were wanted by the pirates, and engaging in a slight dispute with them, the whole crew fell upon and butchered them all. As I was obliged to be a silent spectator of this cruel and most inhuman deed, my blood seemed to congeal in my veins, my pulse to cease its throbbing, and my whole faculties to be paralyzed. But there was no escaping from my situation.

After this slaughter, they took the canoes of the natives, together with their weapons, and expected, thus equipped, to be able to capture some defenceless vessel, when one should heave in sight. Two days elapsed, and a vessel was descried at a distance. It being calm, we all got into the canoes and made towards her. On reaching her, she appeared to be a merchantman, from the African coast, with gold dust and other valuables, and bound for London. On being made acquainted that we had just been shipwrecked, we were received by them and treated with great kindness.

When the pirates had discovered the value of the cargo, a plan was concerted to murder the whole of the vessel's crew, and take possession of the vessel. The moment at length arrived for the insurrection. At a signal they arose, but were promptly met by the vessel's crew, who it seems had been suspicious of their designs all the while. There was a desperate struggle between the parties, but the pirates were at last conquered, without any loss of life. We were all put in chains; but were treated much better than I could have expected. I now considered my destiny fixed, and that no better fate awaited me than death, for there seemed to be no chance of escape. It was thirty-six days before we arrived at London.

Perhaps the reader may imagine in some degree the state of my feelings during the voyage. An orphan, penniless, friendless, and hurdled with a gang of bloody desperadoes, I was confined day and night, and compelled to listen to their blasphemy, as they cursed the protecting hand of heaven, that had arrested them in their guilty career. Though life be desirable, as it is ordinarily possessed, yet I could pray that mine might cease at once, rather than have lived much longer in the situation wherein I was placed. My hand had not been raised against the friendly mariners, by whom we had been so kindly received. My only trust was in Him to whom the most secret thoughts and actions of all are visible.

My limbs were much galled by the irons with which I was bound, yet I did not murmur, though I could hardly stand. My resignation to this hard fate seemed to slightly affect my hardened companions, who knew that I was suffering unjustly. When we arrived at London, we were thrown into damp cells, and there lay several weeks awaiting our trials. At last the eventful time arrived for us to be arraigned. The captain was first tried, and condemned to be hung, then the rest were severally tried, and received the same sentence. Being but a youth, my case was reserved until the last. This was an awful and critical moment for me. Standing before a judge, in the presence of a jury that were sworn to acquit or condemn according to the testimony, I knew my case to be hopeless, unless there should be discovered one spark of pity or humanity in the hearts of the condemned wretches, who were soon to stand before a higher tribunal, and receive the sentence of the Judge of Heaven.

On being asked what I had to say in my behalf, with much emotion I replied, that I was innocent of the crime alleged against me, and that if those that had been condemned could be induced to speak the truth for me, it was all I could ask. After a few moments of breathless silence, during which my destiny was decided, the pirate captain arose, and asking permission, said he had a few words to say before the court proceeded further. He then related how I had come among them, my refusal to participate in their bloody designs, and other particulars in relation to my situation. The mate confirmed the captain's story. By this voluntary act of benevolence on the part of the condemned, I was acquitted and set at liberty. Indeed, my signal deliverance seemed like a miracle performed by Heaven, to signify its regard for truth and justice.

Truly, I did not expect these life giving words from those who had, but a few months before, murdered my companions, and having bound me, were about to add me to the number of their victims. The condemned, nine in all, were solemnly executed. Awful fate! I could not avoid the reflection, of what would be the contrast in their situation, had they like me, made *right* their governing principle, and have partaken of the bitter draught of woe, rather than have quaffed from the poisonous cup of sin.

Again in the streets of London, I wandered about, until I found an opportunity to ship as cook to Boston. We had a pleasant, but rather long voyage. We arrived on the 19th of May, 1794, after I had been absent a considerable time, and had passed through many hardships and hair breadth escapes. I had become weary of this roving life, having neither brother or friend to sympathize with me, in moments of trial, and being constantly alarmed that the character of my sex would be discovered, although by this time I had so well acquired the air and tone of voice of the sailor, that the character seemed familiar to me. I had but a few dollars left after all my hardships, and my health beginning to decline, I kept myself for several days confined, and had abundant time for reflection.

But the more I meditated the worse my situation seemed, and I almost gave myself up to despair. I was not able to labour with men, nor was I skilled in needlework, and having a neglected education, was not qualified to establish a school. I should have sunk under this weight of sorrow, had I not heard many who crossed my path complain of their hard lot, even when they possessed the common comforts and friendships of life. Alas, what would have been their murmurs had they like me been nursed in penury, and rocked in the cradle of affliction! By their ingratitude I gathered new strength, and was resolved at least to be content with my situation, though I should beg for bread from door to door.

One day as I was in search of some employment, and was passing the court-house, I observed a crowd of people pressing in at the door. My curiosity being aroused to learn the cause of this excitement, I placed myself among the mass, and was carried along by the vortex until I reached the court chamber. An involuntary shudder came over me, as I remembered the melancholy fate of those unhappy men, and my own providential deliverance, at a similar tribunal in London. The prisoner had not yet been brought into court. After a while he arrived, attended by an officer; and judge of my horror on recognising in his bloated features, the same Captain Gregory, who attempted my ruin, and who had been the principal cause of all my subsequent sufferings.

The captain, it seems, had become dissipated, and had lost the confidence of his employers. He had in a turn of drunkenness quarrelled with his landlord; of whom he had had his liquor, and killed him. Although the evidence was conclusive against him, his jury rendered a verdict of manslaughter in the first degree. Thus would the wretch probably escape with a few years incarceration in the state prison. But methinks life must be a galling burden to such a being, for conscience, that inward monitor, seldom slumbers in its office, but with an unerring index directs the oblivious memory to its own record of the cankered and guilty soul.

One beautiful morning I went down upon one of the projecting wharves in the harbour. The sun had just arisen. The weather was mild and pleasant, and the view of the harbour was extremely beautiful, there being just enough wind to waft the vessels inward. I was delighted with the calm beauty of nature spread out before me. As I was contemplating these objects, I observed not far from me a gentleman and lady richly clad, with a little girl about three years of age. Their minds appeared to be engrossed with admiration of the beauties spread out before them.

As they strolled along, the child wandered a moment from their side, when suddenly the noise of its fall into the water was heard. So sudden was the transition of their minds from joy to terror, that they stood paralysed by the suddenness of the fearful catastrophe. There was no other person near. I expected the father to plunge in and rescue her. I saw her rise, then sink again, and all was still as the grave; once more she appeared and sank. I resolved to make an effort for her when she again appeared, though I should perish with her. I knew this would be the last opportunity to save her. Her parents in their paroxysms of agony wept aloud. The gurgling of the water now indicated that she was approaching the surface, and for the last time.

Throwing off my jacket, I plunged in, and had the good fortune to catch her as she arose, and placing her in a situation to enable me to swim as well as possible, made my way to a boat, a few rods distant, lifting her into this, I got in myself. Disengaging the boat, I succeeded in mooring it to the wharf, and having landed with my prize, placed it in the arms of its now joyful parents. Their happiness was as sudden and intense as was their grief but a moment before. They showered upon me every possible demonstration of their gratitude. The father tendered to me the contents of his purse, and the lady taking a watch from her side begged me to accept it. But I declined a pecuniary remuneration, and replied, that I had done nothing more than my duty.

Again, I was entreated to accept a reward, as they were wealthy, but I refused, replying that I did not hazard my own life for money. Upon this I was handed their address, and requested, after changing my clothing, to call upon them. I answered, that I should suffer no inconvenience from the water in my clothes; but they insisted that 1 should do as they requested, and call on them in an hour. I nodded assent to the latter proposition, and the gentleman requested me as I passed up the wharf, to send down his carriage which stood at the head of it. I did so.

In about an hour I went by the direction of the card to 91 Tremont street, which appeared an elegant establishment. I rang the door bell, and a servant appeared, of whom I inquired if Mr. Brown was at home, and was answered in the affirmative, but that he was engaged; by this time Mr. Brown had come to the door, and extending his hand, gave me a cordial reception. The child had now so far recovered as to be able to run about. He observed to me, that I had not changed my wet clothes, and seemed apprehensive lest I should get a cold by neglecting it, and thought that I was an obstinate-headed fellow. I told him that was probably the case in some instances. He wished me to explain my meaning. I then made him acquainted with my destitute condition, and that I was not the owner of a change of clothing, and had but a few shillings in the world to buy food with.

This account much excited his compassion, and he inquired next where I lodged. I told him it was with a poor family in an obscure part of the city. He said that I must go with him in a few moments and get a new suit of clothes; this I at first refused, but by his kind solicitations at last consented to receive. I was now informed that a situation would be provided for me in his store, and that I was to live in his family. I told him that such a blunt person as myself would make a ridiculous figure as a member of his family; that being left an orphan at a tender age, and always having to labour hard, I was ashamed of my bad education. I was informed that I should no longer be an orphan, if I would only look upon them as parents and guardians.

Yielding to that powerful instinct in our nature, sympathy, and being intoxicated by the vision of friends and a happy home, I consented to comply with their urgent requests. Their treatment of me was the same as though I had been their child. Their lives were an exemplification of true Christian charity. Having been with them a number of days, I thought best now to come out in my own true colours, and discover who and what I was. But this was a delicate business. I pondered it in my mind for several days, not daring to divulge the whole truth, fearing that they might not credit my story, but think I had disguised myself for some dishonourable purpose. But my virtue and truth I meant to maintain, and if the recital of my history should lessen me in their estimation, and I should be discarded by them, I should at least be as well off as I was before their hospitable reception.

After I had made up my mind to this effect, I was under great anxiety on many accounts, such as how I should appear in a female garb, and how soften the masculine tone my voice had acquired. Not knowing how my story might be received, I obtained one evening, the consent of the family to listen to it after supper. The appointed time came, and with an anxious heart I commenced. I first acquainted them with the poverty, sickness and death of my parents, that I was their only child,—and that child was a female. At the mention of this they started, and looked at me with astonishment. Begging them to calm their emotions, I proceeded with an account of myself while in the Smith family, and the cause of my leaving them, together with every essential particular in my history. They listened with much curiosity and solicitude.

When I had finished, instead of upbraiding me, they showed every mark of tenderness and affection for me. They pledged themselves that I should not want so long as providence was bountiful to them. I now felt the force of his remark, when Mr. Brown called on us to witness, that truth and virtue would in the end vindicate their celestial nature, and come out from the warfare with vice and error unscathed and victorious. I was asked if I should not like to change my dress, for that of a female. I replied that I should be greatly-rejoiced to do so, especially as I had now found protecting friends.

I was soon provided with a stock of rich clothing. My dress now appeared as odd to me as when I first put on male attire. Whilst my hair remained short, I supplied my head with false braids. I was sent to school, and every care taken to make me an ornament in society. Oh what a contrast was this to my situation, when bound by pirates, and death impending over me; or while standing among criminals, awaiting the sentence of their awful doom.

Time passed on, and I had been at my studies about a year and a half. By this time I had worn away my masculine manners, and my voice had assumed its natural tone. One day as I walking down Washington street, in company with Mr. Brown and wife, we noticed a young man on the opposite side staggering about, apparently much intoxicated. As soon as I saw his face, I recognised the person who had attempted my dishonour while I was in the Smith family. I acquainted my benefactors of this, and Mr. Brown accosting a young man with whom he was acquainted, desired him to follow the fellow and ascertain as much as he could in relation to him.

On our return home in a few hours, we found the young man of Mr. Brown's acquaintance, waiting to give us the desired information. He said, that from Washington street he had followed him into several low tippling shops in Hatter's Square, and Ann street, &c. In one of those groggeries he inquired if they knew anything about the fellow, and was informed that he boarded there, or at least received his food for his services in going on errands, and the like for them; that he was a miserable drunkard, and that they should like to be rid of him; that he had been several times in the House of Correction, and that he would be there again soon, and that this was the only fit place for him; that he sometimes got a job of wood sawing, when he was sober.

Mr. Brown was anxious to converse with him, and sent for him to come and saw his wood. He came and commenced his work. After a few moments, Mr. Brown sent word he wished to see him, and desired him to enter the house. He came in, and on being asked if his name was Hackley answered in the affirmative, and that he had long resided in the state of Maine, though he was a native of the state of New York. He was asked if he was ever acquainted with a poor family by the name of Cole. He said he once knew such a family, in which was an only daughter; that the parents were dead; that no one knew anything about the child, except that shortly after her disappearance one night from her adopted home, intelligence was received that she had reached a poor widow's cottage late on one rainy night.

I now asked him if he could inform us of the cause of her singular conduct? At this question he cast a wild glance at me, and for sometime was silent. I thought he had recognised me. Breaking silence, with a deep sigh, he replied that *he* was the only soul that knew the cause—but that he would that the grave had closed over him ere he had become acquainted with it. I asked him if he thought he should recognise her if he could see her. He said he thought he should; but that she must have died long since. On being asked if he would like to see her, he said it would afford him the greatest pleasure.

Mr. Brown now called me by name, and desired me to advance towards them, and pointing at me, said that I was the young orphan in question. Upon this he fell senseless to the floor. Restoratives being applied, he gradually revived; and looking wildly around, he imagined he had been in a dream. At length, perceiving the reality of his situation, he fell at my feet, confessed that he had tried his utmost to ruin me, and because he could not succeed, had been the cause of my being turned out of doors. He beseeched, he entreated me to forgive him. I gave him my forgiveness freely. He confessed that nothing had prospered with him, but that he had been cursed of God ever since that event. Asking our consent to give a brief sketch of his life, he commenced:—

My parents, during my minority, resided in New York. They had always been in comfortable circumstances; and a large legacy from a rich relative in England placed them in an affluent condition. But the suddenness of the possession of this fortune caused them to squander it away in fashionable amusements, and a thousand other vanities. My father at length being awakened to a sense of the state of his sinking fortune, resolved to remove from a society among whom he could not much longer maintain his former station. He accordingly removed to the state of Maine, and engaged in the lumber business. I had two sisters, who with my mother, felt, when they departed eastward, that they had forsaken the world, and were leaving behind them all that makes life desirable.

On arriving in Maine, my father entered largely in the trade of lumber, and in a few years acquired considerable wealth. Myself and sisters were indulged in idleness, and were much pampered by our parents. I grew vain, and was indignant at any effort to oppose my desires. When my attempt of violence upon your person had failed, I resolved to ruin your character, that you might not expose me, and accordingly was the author of that hellish plot by which you was turned out of doors. I exulted for a while, but remorse soon followed, and conscience was ever reminding me what a merciless wretch I had been. Though repentance came, it was too late to undo what had passed. In about two years both of my parents died, leaving me considerable property. I went into business, but every speculation I made turned out badly.

It seemed that a curse rested upon me. I then took to the accursed wine cup, in order to drown my sorrows. I now made worse speculations than ever, and my fortune was nearly gone; when one day being much intoxicated, advantage was taken of my situation, and I was induced to endorse a note for several thousand dollars, and before its maturity the maker failed, and everything being taken from me, I found myself several hundred dollars in debt. Now I was penniless, now I was friendless; for what friends I had not estranged by ill treatment, left me at this last blow. I hung around the grogshops as long as I could be allowed. A vessel coming to Boston, some townsmen offered to pay my passage if I would quit the place, and not let them see me for at least a year. I consented, though not without a small sense of shame at my degraded situation.

I traced the source of all this misery to the injury I had inflicted upon you. But I had only tasted of the bitter draught that was preparing for me. We arrived in Boston, and wandering about until it was nearly night, seeking employment but finding none, I began to ponder on my wretched situation, and coming to a place where temptation is held out to the poor inebriate, I could not resist the enticing draught, which I took, and taking a few cents from my remaining shilling, cast them down and departed.

At length I obtained lodging and board at a cheap establishment, and worked whenever people would employ me, which was only when I was sober, and that was rarely the case. I dragged along for a while in this way, being scarcely able to pay my board, and find myself in liquor. My appetite for strong drink increasing, I gave way to it, and attended to but little business. I could not now pay my board and supply the cravings of my appetite for strong drink, and becoming indebted for them both, I was twice arraigned as a vagabond and drunkard at the bar of your police, and sent to the House of Correction. I made no complaint against your municipal laws, though it seemed rather hard to me that such inducements to dissipation and ruin should be so publicly sanctioned. Alas, I have ruined myself, and there is not the least hope left me. But I ought not complain, for the just visitings of God are upon me.

And concluding his brief narrative, he buried his face in his hands, and wept tears of repentance. I could not help feeling compassion for him under this load of misery, notwithstanding he had been the cause of all my woes. But for him I might never have wanted friends, and a home? Yet the hand that had supported me, compelled him to partake

175

of the bitter draught he had prepared for me, and drain it even to the dregs. He was now broken-hearted and penitent.

My benefactors were touched with compassion at the sight of so much misery, and procured him a boarding place. But his diseased and wrecked frame did not support itself only about a month after this. As he lay upon his death-bed he sent for us to come and see him. When we entered the room, he took me by his cold and death-like hand and again besought me to forgive him. I replied, that I had long since done so. His features brightening, he thanked me and exclaimed:—

Oh do not forsake the path of virtue, and you will surely be happy. Oh that I had never forsaken it; alas, the way of the transgressor is hard. There is no peace to the wicked. Would that I could live my life over again. But it is too late. I shall soon be before my Judge, and receive my due reward.

His horrid features betrayed the most intense agony of mind; a few more convulsions, and he passed into eternity. As I gave a parting glance at his lifeless remains, soon to be returned to their mother earth, I could not forbear the reflection of what would have been his present situation, had he fulfilled the objects of existence designed by his Creator, and been an instrument of good rather than evil to those around him, and a blessing to himself.

Time passed happily on, and I was much respected and beloved by my adopted parents. At length I became acquainted with a young man by the name of Hanson. I noticed a growing attachment on his part for me, and observing a similar feeling increasing with myself, I resolved to put an end to the intimacy. He begged permission to address me, but I declined, saying that I was but a poor orphan, and that he was rich and had been reared in a different rank of society from myself that being affluent and handsome he could have his choice among the many thousand fair ones; that by wedding me he might regret his choice, and I advised him to abandon the thought. He replied, "If that is the case let me have my choice, for you are the one and only one I should select, and to no one else could I offer my heart." He wished me to meditate on it, and consult my friends. On making my new parents acquainted with all that had transpired, they extolled him highly, and encouraged our union; and in about four months we were married.

I lived in wedlock happy and content. Providence blest our union with four children. Thirty-three years of married life passed smoothly away, and we had not a sorrow to mar our happiness. It had always been my study and delight to train up my offspring in the paths of virtue and uprightness, instilling early into their young minds the importance of obeying the divine commands, and the fearful consequences of the least disobedience.

It is with mingled emotions of pleasure and pain that I look back on my past life. The path of my early years was indeed strewn with thorns; and along its mazy and rugged labyrinth I can descry yawning pits, into which I should inevitably have been engulfed, had not virtue been my guide, constantly admonishing me of the impending dangers by which I was surrounded. Yet I put my trust in my heavenly Father. I am now in the vale of years. My children have all married, and are prospering. Having exposed myself to so, many hardships while young, I feel that my health is fast declining, and that I must soon quit the busy stage of life. I have now accomplished the object I had long desired, that of laying before the youth of both sexes, a brief narrative of my life, in which they may see, that however well vice and wrongdoing may prosper for a time, in the end it brings its own woe; and that virtue alone can guard and render them happy in this world, and secure their felicity in another.

Mrs. Emma Hanson died at the age of fifty-nine years and seven months, at her residence in Boston, and her loss was much lamented by a large circle of friends, to whom she was affectionately endeared.